"You don't lose your rights when you clock in. You don't surrender your body when you take a job."— Wayne C. Robinson

Also by Wayne C. Robinson

Enemies Within Us

The Hulda Clark Story

The USAID Scandal: How Billions Disappeared

Why Black Americans No Longer Need DEI

USAID And Child Trafficking

COVID 19 Lawsuits: How to Sue Your Employer And Win

America is $37 Trillion in Debt

Unfit to lead– The End of The Democratic Party

Black Fatigue

The Red Shift: Communism in The U.S.

The 2025 Real State of Black America

Die Hulda Clark Story

The Job Hunt is a Scam: Here's How to Beat It

The Sanctuary City Scam And Black Americans

The Global Black MLM Trap

2026 The Year the Democratic Party Collapses

The Global Black MLM/Network Marketing Trap

Faith, Migration & Power

Lifestyle Red Alert

Everything About Timeshares

Cancel Your Timeshare Today

Everything About Timeshares (2025 Edition)

The Tandem Methods™

She is Africa

Watch for more at www.enemieswithinus.com.

COVID Mandate Lawsuits: How to Sue Your Employer and Win

How to Demand Back Pay, Emotional Damages, and Punitive Compensation from Your Employer

By

Wayne C. Robinson

For permissions or inquiries, contact:

Wayne Robinson Productions

contactus@www.enemieswithinus.com

Legal Disclaimer

This book is for informational and educational purposes only. The author and publisher are not attorneys, medical professionals, or financial advisors. The content in this book is not intended as legal, medical, or financial advice and should not be used as a substitute for professional guidance.

While every effort has been made to ensure the accuracy of the information contained herein, laws and legal interpretations vary by jurisdiction and are subject to change. Readers are encouraged to consult with qualified legal professionals regarding their specific employment and wrongful termination cases. The author and publisher assume no responsibility for errors, omissions, or liabilities incurred as a result of the use of this book.

The names of individuals and companies mentioned in this book may be real or fictionalized to protect privacy. Any resemblance to actual persons, living or dead, is purely coincidental.

First Edition: 2025

Introduction

In the ever-evolving landscape of workplace dynamics, 2020 brought changes that no one could have anticipated. At the forefront was an unprecedented global health crisis, altering not only our personal lives but also fundamentally reshaping employment as we knew it. As governments and corporations raced to manage the public health emergency, vaccine mandates emerged as a divisive issue, sparking fierce debate over individual rights versus collective health responsibilities. This book delves into these turbulent times, offering a voice to those who faced wrongful terminations because of their personal medical choices.

As the pandemic unfolded, companies and government agencies were quick to enforce vaccine compliance measures—a decision that has since led to mass terminations. Many employees found themselves at a crossroads, forced to choose between maintaining their livelihoods and adhering to their convictions about bodily autonomy. In this book, we uncover the stories of those who were confronted with such life-altering decisions, providing a platform for their voices to be heard amidst the clamor of corporate and governmental directives.

For healthcare workers and first responders—the nurses, doctors, hospital staff, police officers, firefighters, and military personnel—the choice often seemed insurmountable. Esteemed professionals, once hailed as heroes, suddenly faced discharge or being sidelined for refusing the jab. This narrative is not just a chronicle of policy enforcement; it's an exploration of courage, conviction, and the pursuit of justice in the face of adversity.

While the world grappled with its pandemic response, new evidence began emerging, challenging the efficacy and safety of rapid vaccine deployment. News of adverse reactions and vaccine-related injuries started to surface, lending complexity to an already convoluted dialogue. The book dives into these developments, shedding light on the legal rights employees now possess—rights that many were unaware of when facing unjust dismissal.

Central to this work is the critical issue of wrongful termination due to COVID-19 mandates. This book does more than merely recount the hardships; it seeks to empower. With detailed guidance on pursuing legal recourse, wrongfully terminated employees can find tangible steps to fight back against what they believe were unconstitutional demands. By dissecting major lawsuits where employees successfully defended their right to refuse vaccination, we illustrate paths to triumph, inspiring others to consider possible legal avenues.

But the impact extends beyond individuals—the ripple effects touch families, too. The spouses, parents, and children of those who lost jobs grapple with financial instability and emotional upheaval. The narratives within these pages highlight the social and economic repercussions felt by entire households, painting a fuller picture of how enforced mandates reverberate through communities.

Our exploration includes the experiences of those who, despite initial compliance under coercion, later regretted their choices. For them, questions linger: Can justice still be sought? Is there hope for redress? This book offers insights into potential legal actions available even after compliance—journeys that reveal both pitfalls and promising strategies.

Vaccine-injured individuals add another layer to the conversation. Their stories speak of unforeseen medical complications post-vaccination and the struggle to navigate medical bureaucracy while advocating against further imposition of mandates. These personal accounts raise urgent questions about informed consent and the ethical implications of government-imposed medical decisions.

Legal and labor rights advocates play a pivotal role in this discourse. Employment attorneys and activists tirelessly challenge unlawful policies and fight for the protection of free will. Their work underscores the resilience inherent in individuals who refuse to accept blanket mandates without scrutiny. Throughout the book, we engage with these leaders, exploring how their efforts contribute to broader calls for maintaining personal freedoms in the workforce.

The political dimension cannot be ignored. Conservatives, libertarians, independents, and other like-minded individuals rally around the belief that governmental overreach infringes upon constitutional rights. In exploring these perspectives, the book captures a diverse array of voices united by a common cause: opposing mandates viewed as intrusions on personal liberty.

Finally, whistleblowers and investigative researchers bring essential clarity to the narrative. Their commitment to exposing potential fraud behind COVID-19 mandates and policies uncovers layers of complexity that demand closer examination. Through their dedication, we gain a deeper understanding of the mechanisms driving these far-reaching decisions.

In bringing together these multifaceted stories, this book aims to shed light on an era marked by profound upheaval in employment law and personal rights. We invite readers to journey with us, traversing the landscapes of legal battles, personal stories, and ongoing efforts to uphold freedom in the face of daunting challenges. Here, wrongfully terminated workers and their allies find solidarity and strength, guided by the hope that justice can indeed prevail.

Part I: The COVID-19 Vaccine Mandate and Legal Fallout

Chapter 1 How the COVID-19 Vaccine Mandates Violated Employee Rights

The impact of COVID-19 vaccine mandates on employee rights has been a contentious issue, eliciting strong reactions from various sectors of society. As government agencies, private corporations, and healthcare facilities enforced these mandates, they encountered both support and resistance. The ensuing debate touched on fundamental topics such as personal freedom, public health, and workplace safety. In navigating this complex terrain, employees faced significant challenges, grappling with the implications of mandatory vaccination on their autonomy and job security.

This chapter delves into the multifaceted consequences of vaccine mandates, exploring how different organizations approached enforcement in diverse socioeconomic contexts. From government agencies implementing broad policies to private companies prioritizing business continuity and healthcare facilities safeguarding patient safety, each sector presented unique dynamics. The chapter also examines the legal and ethical debates sparked by these mandates, highlighting the tension between institutional objectives and individual rights. Furthermore, it sheds light on the broader societal impacts, including economic repercussions and shifts in public perception, as people weighed personal choice against collective responsibility. By unpacking these themes, the chapter offers a comprehensive overview of the intricate interplay between vaccine mandates and employee rights during the pandemic era.

Enforcement of Vaccine Requirements by Various Entities

The enforcement of COVID-19 vaccine mandates by different organizations presents a complex landscape, reflecting the diversity of values, priorities, and legal frameworks within government agencies, private corporations, and healthcare facilities. Analyzing how these institutions implemented their mandates provides insights into the varied impacts on employee rights and workplace dynamics.

Government agencies were at the forefront of shaping nationwide policies on COVID-19 vaccinations. These entities implemented strict guidelines to ensure public health safety, often setting standards that other sectors were encouraged or mandated to follow. For example, in many countries, government mandates required public sector employees to be vaccinated as a condition for continued employment. This approach was primarily driven by the need to maintain uninterrupted public services and protect vulnerable populations from COVID-19 outbreaks. The impact of these mandates, however, sparked significant debates about personal freedoms versus collective safety, illustrating the fundamental tension between individual rights and public responsibilities. Government interventions were often seen as benchmarks for private sectors, serving as a template for similar policies across various industries (Flood, 2021).

In tandem with government efforts, private corporations introduced vaccine mandates aimed at safeguarding workplace health and ensuring business continuity. Many companies viewed vaccination as crucial for preventing disruptions caused by COVID-19 outbreaks, which could lead to operational slowdowns or temporary closures. For instance, major firms, particularly those in retail and manufacturing, adopted vaccine requirements as part of their strategy to reduce transmission risks among employees and customers. These mandates were supported by scientific evidence indicating that vaccines significantly lowered the risk of severe illness and transmission. Nevertheless, they also led to disputes over employment rights, with some employees resisting mandates on grounds of medical, religious, or personal beliefs. Legal challenges in various jurisdictions tested the boundaries of corporate mandates, focusing on whether employers could lawfully require vaccination without infringing upon individual liberties (Healthcare Employers and Vaccine Mandates, 2021).

Healthcare facilities, perhaps more than any other sector, prioritized patient safety through compulsory vaccination policies for staff. The rationale was clear: healthcare workers are at a higher risk of exposure to COVID-19, and unvaccinated staff could pose a direct threat to patients, especially those who are immunocompromised or critically ill. As a result, numerous hospitals and clinics mandated vaccinations to protect both their workforce and the patients in their care. These facilities had a compelling ethical obligation to minimize the spread of the virus, aligning with broader public health imperatives. Despite the logical basis for such mandates, they also resulted in resistance from some healthcare professionals, raising concerns about autonomy and informed consent. The friction between institutional objectives and personal choice highlighted ongoing challenges in balancing public health goals with individual rights (Frati, 2021).

Variations in enforcement of vaccine mandates led to diverse impacts on employees across different sectors, underscoring the complexity of implementing uniform policies in a diverse socioeconomic landscape. In some industries, mandates were strictly enforced, resulting in penalties or termination for non-compliance, while others adopted more flexible approaches, allowing for exemptions and alternative safety measures like regular testing. This inconsistency sometimes fostered confusion and resentment among employees, who perceived inequitable treatment in mandate applications. Moreover, sectors such as transportation and education faced unique challenges due to high public interaction, necessitating carefully crafted policies to ensure both compliance and employee satisfaction. The differential impacts of mandates on various workforces have sparked discussions on equity and fairness, raising questions about the proportionality of mandates concerning the risks faced by different groups (Kates, 2021).

"No Jab, No Job" Policies and Their Impact

The enforcement of COVID-19 vaccine mandates in workplaces has had far-reaching consequences, impacting not only individual employees but also broader economic and legal landscapes.

One of the immediate effects of these mandates was job insecurity. As organizations required vaccinations for continued employment, many employees found themselves at a crossroads. Particularly vulnerable were those working on non-standard contracts or in industries heavily impacted by the pandemic. Such policies exacerbated fears of unemployment, as workers who were unwilling or unable to comply faced potential termination (Moore et al., 2024). This situation led to increased anxiety and uncertainty among employees, which further strained mental health during an already challenging period.

In this turbulent landscape, workers were often forced to choose between career stability and personal health autonomy. For some, complying with the mandate meant consenting to medical procedures they were uncomfortable with. Others stood firm in their decision to forgo vaccination due to personal beliefs or health concerns, risking their jobs in the process. The pressure to conform created a dilemma that tested individual resolve and highlighted the complex interactions between workplace requirements and personal freedoms (Politis et al., 2023).

Legal challenges quickly emerged as a significant aftermath of these mandates. Many employees, believing their rights were being violated, turned to the courts for relief. Lawsuits claimed wrongful termination and discrimination, questioning the legality of forcing employees into making such personal decisions under duress. These legal battles not only underscored the contentious nature of the mandates but also highlighted divisions in public opinion regarding the balance between public health measures and individual liberties. Courts across various jurisdictions were tasked with navigating these unprecedented cases, setting precedents that would influence future employment policies.

Beyond individual struggles, the economic repercussions of vaccine mandates rippled through larger market dynamics. Organizations faced operational disruptions as they grappled with staff shortages resulting from employee departures or terminations. Industries that were already facing labor shortages found themselves in even more precarious situations. The healthcare sector, for example, experienced intensified staffing challenges, affecting its ability to deliver services effectively (Politis et al., 2023).

Moreover, the mandates influenced market behaviors by impacting consumer confidence and spending. Businesses, particularly in sectors like hospitality and retail, dealt with fluctuations in workforce availability, leading to reduced service offerings and adjusted business hours. As a result, local economies felt the strain, affecting everything from small enterprises to large corporations. The mandates inadvertently accelerated trends such as remote work and automation, as companies sought ways to circumvent staffing issues and maintain productivity.

The intersection of race and class also played a crucial role in how these mandates were perceived and resisted. Marginalized communities, disproportionately represented in essential worker roles, faced heightened risks. Often employed in positions that afforded little flexibility or bargaining power, these workers' experiences were informed by systemic inequalities that predated the pandemic. Policies that might appear neutral on the surface had disparate impacts based on existing social and economic disparities (Moore et al., 2024).

Initial Public Response to Vaccine Mandates

The early reactions to COVID-19 vaccine mandates were marked by widespread skepticism, which ignited debates about individual liberties versus public health. This skepticism arose from mistrust in governmental decisions about personal health and the speed at which vaccines were developed and mandated. Many people questioned the balance between protecting public health and respecting individual rights to make medical choices. This tension was particularly pronounced among those who felt coerced into compliance, fearing overreach by authorities (Bolsen & Palm, 2021).

Public protests became a visible manifestation of this division, highlighting societal rifts regarding mandatory vaccination. Demonstrations erupted globally, with participants voicing concerns over bodily autonomy and government mandates. These protests underscored the varying perspectives on vaccination—not only as a health issue but as a question of personal freedom.

The intensity of these protests reflected deep-rooted fears and values across different societal groups, hinting at a broader cultural clash.

Acceptance levels of the mandates varied significantly, illustrating differing cultural and social perceptions. In some communities, vaccination accepted as a critical health measure; in others, it sparked resistance based on historical distrust of government or past injustices. For instance, Black and Latino communities exhibited hesitancy due to longstanding medical exploitation and inequities, affecting their response to mandates (Pennington, 2021). Simultaneously, more liberal areas tended to show higher acceptance, viewing mandates as a societal duty. This mixed acceptance portrays a complex web of beliefs shaped by cultural identity, personal experiences, and socio-economic backgrounds.

The media played a crucial role in shaping opinions and disseminating information about vaccine mandates. With the rapid spread of information—and misinformation—through digital channels, people's views were swayed by the narratives they consumed. Media outlets across the spectrum contributed to the polarized discourse, either supporting mandates as necessary public health measures or framing them as infringements on freedom. The proliferation of conspiracy theories further complicated this landscape, with some partisans using media platforms to amplify baseless claims and foster fear. As such, media consumption became a significant factor in how individuals processed and responded to mandates (Bolsen & Palm, 2021).

One study highlighted the profound impact of scientific messaging on public perception. When individuals were exposed to messages communicating the consensus among scientists regarding vaccine safety, resistance decreased notably (Bolsen & Palm, 2021). This finding underscores media's power in informing or misinforming the public. It also points to the importance of accurate, transparent communication from trusted sources to counteract skepticism.

Despite attempts to reduce misunderstandings, correcting misinformation proved challenging. Research indicated that while factual corrections improved some people's accuracy on COVID-related issues, they did not have lasting effects on eradicating false beliefs entirely (Bolsen & Palm, 2021). This suggests that deeply ingrained ideologies and identity-based thinking often override objective facts. Therefore, achieving a widespread understanding of vaccine mandates' necessity requires strategic communication efforts tailored to specific audiences.

Evolving Attitudes with New Medical Revelations

As the COVID-19 vaccine mandates were rolled out, public opinion underwent significant evolution. This subpoint delves into the shifts in perception as new information surfaced over time. One of the primary catalysts for this change was scientific advancements, which continuously updated people's understanding of vaccine efficacy and safety. Initially, there was considerable skepticism about how well the vaccines could protect against COVID-19. Reports highlighting their effectiveness against severe illness and death gradually helped in shifting opinions towards acceptance (World Health Organization, 2021). The dissemination of clear, factual information by credible scientific bodies was crucial in altering the narrative around vaccine safety concerns.

Beyond scientific breakthroughs, revised healthcare protocols further influenced public acceptance and compliance with vaccine mandates. As the pandemic unfolded, health organizations adapted their strategies to respond better to emerging challenges. These adaptations included updating vaccination guidelines based on real-time data, which empowered healthcare professionals to address public concerns more effectively. With each update, individuals began to see the rationale behind mandates more clearly, realizing these measures were not arbitrary impositions but part of a dynamic response to a global health crisis (Welch et al., 2023).

Moreover, the growing awareness of the societal benefits associated with widespread vaccination played a pivotal role in reducing resistance to vaccine policies. While individual freedoms remained a point of contention, the collective benefit of achieving herd immunity became widely recognized. Public health campaigns emphasized not only personal protection but also the broader impact on community health, stressing how vaccines could curb transmission rates and prevent healthcare systems from being overwhelmed. This shift in messaging highlighted the interconnectedness of society and encouraged people to view vaccination as a social responsibility rather than a mere personal choice.

The ongoing dialogue between experts and the public further facilitated more informed perspectives. In the early stages of the pandemic, misinformation spread rapidly, creating confusion and fear. However, as experts engaged more openly through various media channels, they provided clarity on vaccine-related queries. Platforms such as webinars, interviews, and Q&A sessions allowed scientists to communicate directly with the public, dispelling myths and correcting falsehoods. This steady stream of expert insights cultivated trust and encouraged more individuals to base their decisions on facts rather than hearsay (Welch et al., 2023).

In tracking these changes in public opinion, it's evident that transparency in scientific communication and progressive healthcare strategies were instrumental in addressing vaccine hesitancy. The initial reluctance, underscored by fears of unknown side effects and distrust in rapid vaccine development, was mitigated by evidence-backed reassurances. As more data emerged showcasing the success of vaccination programs worldwide, perceptions shifted from skepticism to cautious optimism.

Social influences also played a considerable role in shaping public attitudes. Individuals who initially resisted vaccination due to peer pressure or misinformation found themselves reconsidering after observing positive outcomes among vaccinated peers. Testimonials from trusted community figures and influencers further swayed opinions, reinforcing the message that getting vaccinated was a step toward returning to normalcy.

Concluding Thoughts

As we conclude this chapter, we've delved into the complexities surrounding COVID-19 vaccine mandates and their impact on employee rights. It's clear that these mandates sparked wide-ranging debates over personal freedoms, legalities, and public health responsibilities. Government agencies and private corporations adopted varying approaches, from strict enforcement to more flexible policies, leading to a patchwork of experiences across different sectors. Employees faced dilemmas between maintaining job security and protecting their health autonomy, highlighting personal and societal tensions. The resulting legal battles not only tested employment laws but also reflected broader public challenges in balancing safety with individual liberties.

These mandates have left a significant economic and social imprint. Industries already struggling with labor shortages encountered further difficulties due to staff departures and terminations. The effects were felt deeply by marginalized communities, who often bore the brunt of these policies. Public skepticism and protests underscored the complexity of implementing such mandates, while evolving scientific insights gradually shifted perceptions towards acceptance. This chapter has provided insight into the layered implications of vaccine requirements, urging us to consider how future policies might balance public health needs with respect for personal choices.

Reference List

Bolsen, T., & Palm, R. (2021, November 10). Politicization and COVID-19 vaccine resistance in the U.S. Progress in Molecular Biology and Translational Science. https://doi.org/10.1016/bs.pmbts.2021.10.002

Healthcare Employers And Vaccine Mandates. (2021). Parsonsbehle.com. https://parsonsbehle.com/insights/Healthcare-Employers-Vaccine-Mandates

Moore, S., Amendah, E. R., Clamp, C., Carter, N., Burns, C., & Martin, W. (2024, February 1). Understanding vaccine hesitancy in US and UK frontline workers – The role of economic risk. Safety Science; Elsevier BV. https://doi.org/10.1016/j.ssci.2023.106350

Maneze, D., Salamonson, Y., Grollman, M., Montayre, J., & Ramjan, L. (2022, November 9). Mandatory COVID-19 vaccination for healthcare workers: A systematic review. International Journal of Nursing Studies. https://doi.org/10.1016/j.ijnurstu.2022.104389

Pennington, M. (2021, July 29). History of Vaccine Hesitancy. Charles River. https://www.criver.com/eureka/history-vaccine-hesitancy

Politis, M., Sotiriou, S., Doxani, C., Stefanidis, I., Zintzaras, E., & Rachiotis, G. (2023, April 21). Healthcare Workers' Attitudes towards Mandatory COVID-19 Vaccination: A Systematic Review and Meta-Analysis. Vaccines. https://doi.org/10.3390/vaccines11040880

World Health Organization. (2021, July 14). Vaccine efficacy, Effectiveness and Protection. World Health Organisation. https://www.who.int/news-room/feature-stories/detail/vaccine-efficacy-effectiveness-and-protection

Welch, E. W., Johnson, T. P., Chen, T., Ma, J., Islam, S., Michalegko, L. F., Caldarulo, M., & Frandell, A. (2023, July 6). How Scientists View Vaccine Hesitancy. Vaccines. https://doi.org/10.3390/vaccines11071208

Chapter 2 The Legal Framework for Fighting Back

Navigating the legal framework for combating wrongful termination is an intricate endeavor, especially when vaccine mandates enter the scene. The ever-evolving dynamics of employment law have taken on new dimensions in response to public health directives, propelling both employees and employers into a complex landscape. For workers faced with termination or compliance dilemmas, understanding these legal structures has become crucial. Amidst ongoing debates, uncovering the layers of protection available against wrongful dismissal can provide invaluable insights. This chapter sits at the intersection of personal rights and mandatory policies, revealing how these elements coexist within today's legal systems.

Throughout this chapter, readers will delve into the multifaceted components that form the backbone of wrongful termination laws, particularly as they relate to exceptions and mandates. It draws upon case studies and real-world examples to illustrate common scenarios and legal precedents that inform current practices. Discussion will highlight the subtle interplay between collective bargaining agreements, statutory protections, and judicial interpretations, detailing their influence on the issue at hand. By examining exemptions and the roles played by religious and medical considerations, this exploration seeks to illuminate effective strategies for navigating these issues. Readers gain clarity on pursuing claims and defending rights within the shifting terrain of employment law, providing a comprehensive guide to addressing these modern challenges.

Understanding Wrongful Termination Laws and Vaccine Mandates

The intersection of wrongful termination laws and vaccine mandates is complex and multifaceted, as it delves into the complexities of employment law in light of evolving public health directives. Wrongful termination generally refers to a situation where an employee has been let go from their job in a manner that breaches legal or contractual stipulations. This could involve firing someone without the proper reasoning dictated by an employment contract, or contravening statutory protections. Within the current climate, where vaccine mandates became prevalent due to the COVID-19 pandemic, these traditional definitions are being tested and reshaped.

The pandemic ushered in unprecedented challenges for both employers and employees. Vaccine mandates, aimed at promoting public health, also introduced dilemmas regarding individual rights and employment security. These mandates have seen many employers requiring vaccination as a condition for continued employment, sparking debates around wrongful termination. Workers argue that such dismissals often retaliate against employees who exercise their right to medical autonomy or who seek exemptions on various grounds.

Employees facing termination over vaccine mandates have contended that such actions can amount to retaliation, particularly when related to health-related mandates. This argument stems from scenarios where workers perceive their terminations as a consequence of asserting their rights, whether those rights pertain to requests for accommodation due to medical conditions, religious beliefs, or personal convictions. These cases often highlight the nuances in balancing public health interests with individual freedoms, a debate that continues to evolve in legal contexts.

Legal protections against unjust dismissals exist under various federal, state, and local statutes designed to safeguard employees' rights. For instance, in New York City, the Human Rights Law prohibits wrongful termination based on discriminatory practices. Employees terminated under suspect circumstances can pursue claims if they believe such action was due to their membership in protected classes or based on other legal grounds (Lipsky Lowe LLP, 2024).

These protections underline the necessity of ensuring fair treatment and underscore the employer's responsibility to adhere to lawful processes.

Moreover, collective bargaining agreements play a pivotal role in this landscape, particularly for unionized workers. Such agreements may contain specific provisions safeguarding against layoffs without cause, providing additional layers of protection. If these provisions are breached, affected employees might be entitled to remedies outlined in their agreements. During the pandemic, there were instances where blanket layoffs were used to mask discriminatory practices, which further complicated the issue of wrongful termination.

Employers are cautioned to execute any mandate-related terminations uniformly and transparently to mitigate risks of wrongful termination lawsuits. The key lies in documenting decisions clearly and ensuring equal application across all employees. Courts have weighed in on these matters, with rulings highlighting the importance of consistent decision-making processes and the avoidance of arbitrary enforcement of health mandates (Will Ending Vaccine Mandates Expose Employers to Lawsuits? | WorldatWork, 2023).

Understanding wrongful termination laws and how they apply to vaccine mandates involves navigating these complex issues. Employing entities must ensure compliance with prevailing labor laws while weighing the nuances involved in mandating vaccines. Legal guidance often becomes crucial in these situations, helping both employers and employees navigate potential disputes swiftly and effectively.

Religious Exemption Claims under Title VII

Understanding religious exemption claims under Title VII of the Civil Rights Act is essential for those navigating the legal landscape shaped by vaccine mandates. Title VII aims to prevent employment discrimination by compelling employers to accommodate employees' sincerely held religious beliefs unless such accommodations result in undue hardship on business operations. This framework presents a complex arena where personal beliefs intersect with public health policies.

Title VII's anti-discrimination provisions explicitly include religion, mandating that employers cannot treat employees unfavorably based on their religious beliefs or practices. This protection extends to preventing job termination when an employee requests an exemption from workplace policies that conflict with their religious convictions. For instance, during the COVID-19 pandemic, many employees sought religious exemptions from vaccine mandates implemented by their employers. Under Title VII, these employees are entitled to request reasonable accommodations, provided their belief systems meet the conditions of being sincerely held (Mello & Parmet, 2023).

However, not all claims for religious exemptions are automatically valid. The sincerity of religious beliefs often becomes a focal point in determining eligibility for exemptions. Unlike personal or secular beliefs, which do not qualify under Title VII, religious beliefs must be bona fide and deeply held. This requires more than merely articulating a religious stance; it involves demonstrating that the beliefs are genuine and part of a broader religious practice. Legal interpretations have upheld that these beliefs can evolve over time, reflecting changing spiritual understandings rather than static doctrines (Ong, 2024).

Employers facing requests for religious accommodations must thoroughly assess whether providing such accommodations would impose an undue hardship. The Supreme Court's decision in Groff v. DeJoy shifted the definition of undue hardship from a minimal burden to one that causes substantial strain on business resources or operations. This significant change implies that employers must explore numerous possibilities to facilitate accommodation without straightforwardly denying requests based on perceived inconveniences (Mello & Parmet, 2023).

The recent ruling reinforces that economic considerations are central to assessing undue hardship. It necessitates evaluating the financial impact of accommodating religious beliefs against maintaining effective business operations. For example, in healthcare settings, where patient safety may be compromised by unvaccinated staff, courts may favor vaccine mandates unless considerable evidence supports alternative measures to ensure safety without service disruption.

Legal precedents continue to shape how religious exemptions are interpreted within the context of workplace demands. Courts frequently reference past judgments, contributing to a growing body of case law guiding employers' decision-making processes. The outcome of cases like Groff v. DeJoy demonstrates the judiciary's evolving perspective on religious accommodations, urging employers to carefully document and justify the potential hardships claimed.

Employers are increasingly advised to maintain robust records documenting requests for religious exemptions, noting how decisions align with both legal requirements and organizational policies. Transparency in this procedure not only fosters trust but also mitigates risks related to potential litigation. Employers should engage in dialogue with employees, exploring alternatives that could satisfy both the religious obligations of employees and operational necessities.

Healthcare institutions, major stakeholders impacted by these developments, must balance public health priorities with respect for individual religious rights. Crafting and communicating clear, evidence-based vaccination policies helps navigate these legal intricacies while aligning with Title VII's mandates.

Title VII stands as a pivotal element in upholding religious liberty within workplaces, offering a structured avenue for addressing conflicts between faith-based practices and corporate mandates. Its provisions highlight the importance of understanding religious exemptions beyond superficial claims, demanding sincere introspection into what constitutes a core part of one's spiritual identity.

Medical Exemption Claims under ADA Protections

The Americans with Disabilities Act (ADA) plays a crucial role in protecting individuals with disabilities from workplace discrimination. According to the ADA, employers cannot discriminate against employees based on their disabilities. This legal protection extends to medical exemptions from mandatory vaccination programs, provided that an employee can present documented evidence of a disability that contraindicates vaccination.

To meet the requirements for a medical exemption under the ADA, it's necessary to demonstrate that the employee has a legitimate disability that interferes with receiving a vaccine. For instance, individuals who have severe allergic reactions to components in vaccines may have a valid claim. However, this requires adequate documentation from a healthcare provider, confirming that the disability significantly impacts the individual's ability to be vaccinated.

Employers are obligated to provide reasonable accommodations for employees with disabilities unless doing so would cause significant difficulty or expense—known as "undue hardship." The concept of undue hardship is determined case-by-case and considers factors like the nature and cost of the accommodation, the overall financial resources of the employer, and the impact on business operations. An example of reasonable accommodation could include allowing remote work or implementing additional safety measures such as mask-wearing or frequent testing.

Case law provides valuable insights into how the ADA applies to medical exemptions in the context of health mandates, especially amid the COVID-19 pandemic. A noteworthy case involved Ruggiero v. Mount Nittany Medical Center, where an employee claimed severe anxiety regarding a TDAP vaccine as a disabling condition. Though her initial request for accommodation was denied, she argued that wearing a mask instead of receiving the vaccine was a reasonable solution. Ultimately, the court found that the plaintiff had presented sufficient allegations to withstand a motion to dismiss, demonstrating that the courts might recognize anxiety as a valid ADA claim under certain circumstances (Employment Discrimination Claims Related to Vaccination Refusal – Disability, n.d.).

Moreover, the Equal Employment Opportunity Commission (EEOC) has issued guidelines indicating that employers must engage in an interactive process with employees requesting accommodations due to disabilities. This process involves communication between the employer and the employee to explore potential accommodations. Employers should ensure that managers and supervisors are trained to handle such requests and assess them fairly and consistently.

In some instances, medical inquiries and examinations related to vaccinations are permissible if they align with business necessity. Under the ADA, once an employee starts working, any disability-related inquiries or medical exams must be job-related and consistent with that necessity. For example, if an unvaccinated employee poses a direct threat to others' health or safety that cannot be mitigated through reasonable accommodations, the employer may need to consider vaccination status as part of maintaining workplace safety (EEOC, 2020).

Determining whether an unvaccinated employee constitutes a direct threat involves evaluating various factors, including the risk's duration, the harm's severity, the likelihood of occurrence, and its imminence. If a direct threat is identified, employers should then determine if there are feasible accommodations available that do not impose undue hardship. Guidance from public health authorities, such as the CDC and OSHA, can help employers make informed decisions regarding these matters.

For employers implementing vaccination programs, it is important to note that the administration of vaccines does not count as a medical examination under the ADA. However, pre-screening questions that potentially reveal disabilities must be job-related and necessary for business purposes. In voluntary vaccination programs, employers can inquire into vaccination status without needing to meet this standard, but they must remain mindful of employees' privacy rights.

Personal Autonomy and Legal Uncertainty

In the evolving legal landscape, personal autonomy claims have gained significant attention due to ongoing disputes surrounding bodily integrity and vaccine mandates. Personal autonomy underscores the fundamental right of individuals to govern their own bodies and shield themselves from unwanted medical interventions. This principle finds its roots in long-standing legal doctrines that uphold the ability of individuals to make intimate decisions about their health without unwarranted intrusions.

The conversation around personal autonomy is particularly pertinent as governments implemented policies mandating COVID-19 vaccinations for various employment sectors. Many employees have pushed back against these mandates, asserting that such requirements infringe on their personal rights to control their own health decisions. This has led to a surge in legal battles where courts are tasked with balancing individual liberties against public health imperatives.

Legal frameworks addressing bodily integrity are currently in flux, with divergent outcomes emerging across jurisdictions. As different states and countries adopt distinct approaches to handle personal autonomy and public health, inconsistencies in rulings arise. For instance, some states grant more expansive rights to opt out of vaccine mandates on personal autonomy grounds, while others prioritize collective health measures over individual resistance. This patchwork approach highlights the complexity and variability within legal systems, emphasizing the need for clear guidelines.

Court rulings are increasingly being called upon to weigh individual rights against the broader interests of public health. Judicial decisions must navigate the delicate balance between safeguarding an individual's right to refuse medical treatment and protecting community health. In some cases, courts have sided with individuals, recognizing the right to personal autonomy as paramount, while in others they have prioritized the government's responsibility to ensure public safety through vaccination efforts.

A notable example is when courts have ruled in favor of healthcare organizations enforcing vaccine mandates to protect vulnerable patients, even if it means overriding personal autonomy objections from staff. Such decisions illustrate the judicial tendency to respect collective health needs in high-risk environments. Yet, other court decisions have reinforced personal choice, reflecting the judiciary's role as a guardian of individual freedoms.

Looking ahead, future legal clarifications are anticipated as courts continue to adjudicate these nuanced disputes. The ongoing legal battles suggest that interpretations of personal autonomy will evolve, shaped by new precedents and societal values. As courts deliberate this issue further, they may establish stronger standards to reconcile the tension between individual rights and public health imperatives. Such legal developments could pave the way for more consistent jurisprudence across jurisdictions, providing clearer guidance for similar future cases.

The legal contention surrounding personal autonomy and vaccine mandates remains deeply contentious, reflecting broader ideological debates about the boundaries of government intervention in personal health matters. This has been seen not only in the workplace but also in educational institutions and public spaces where vaccine mandates have been enforced more stringently. Legal strategies often involve challenging the mandates based on constitutional grounds, asserting violations of rights like bodily autonomy and privacy.

Amidst these legal battles, there are growing calls for legislative actions that might better define the scope of personal autonomy in the context of public health. Advocates argue for the creation of comprehensive laws that articulate clear criteria under which personal autonomy can be exercised without undermining communal protection measures. Such legislation would aim to harmonize disparate legal interpretations and provide individuals and organizations with a clearer understanding of rights and responsibilities.

Personal autonomy advocacy is bolstered by wider civil liberties movements that champion the preservation of individual freedoms against perceived government overreach. These advocates emphasize the necessity of maintaining human rights principles even when faced with global health crises. Their efforts highlight the importance of thoughtful discourse on how society can navigate the challenges of modern governance, ensuring decisions made in the name of public safety do not erode foundational personal rights.

Ultimately, the legal landscape surrounding personal autonomy and vaccine mandates will likely continue to be dynamic and contentious. As courts confront these issues, they not only shape the immediate future of health regulations but also influence broader societal attitudes toward personal rights and governmental authority. Stakeholders on all sides — from legal experts and policymakers to employers and the general public — await these decisions with keen interest, knowing their implications extend well beyond the courtroom.

Insights and Implications

Throughout this chapter, we've navigated the intricate landscape where wrongful termination laws intersect with vaccine mandates. These issues have sparked heated debates as both employees and employers try to interpret rapidly evolving legal frameworks. We've explored how these mandates pose challenges around individual rights versus public health priorities and how this impacts job security. Legal protections exist to prevent unjust dismissals, but understanding their application requires a detailed look into individual circumstances and relevant statutes. From collective bargaining agreements to local laws like New York City's Human Rights Law, there's a vast spectrum of elements influencing how cases are addressed and resolved.

Our discussion also highlighted key aspects of religious and medical exemptions under Title VII and the ADA, along with personal autonomy considerations. Employers are tasked with balancing employee rights with operational necessities, a complex challenge made even more complicated by differing state and federal guidelines. By delving into these subjects, the chapter aims to equip readers, especially those impacted or concerned about workplace vaccination mandates, with valuable insights. For anyone facing or fearing wrongful termination over vaccine policies, understanding these legal nuances is vital in navigating potential disputes and asserting one's rights effectively.

Reference List

An Eventful Summer for State Constitutional Abortion Rights Litigation. (2024). State Court Report. https://statecourtreport.org/our-work/analysis-opinion/eventful-summer-state-constitutional-abortion-rights-litigation

Employment Discrimination Claims Related to Vaccination Refusal – Disability. (n.d.). Www.whiteandwilliams.com. https://www.whiteandwilliams.com/resources-alerts-Disability-Employment-Discrimination-Claims-Related-to-Vaccination-Refusal

EEOC. (2020, December 16). What You Should Know About COVID-19 and the ADA, the Rehabilitation Act, and Other EEO Laws | U.S. Equal Employment Opportunity Commission. Www.eeoc.gov. https://www.eeoc.gov/wysk/what-you-should-know-about-covid-19-and-ada-rehabilitation-act-and-other-eeo-laws

Felix, M., & Sobel, L. (2023, January 20). Legal Challenges to State Abortion Bans Since the Dobbs Decision. KFF. https://www.kff.org/womens-health-policy/issue-brief/legal-challenges-to-state-abortion-bans-since-the-dobbs-decision/

Lipsky Lowe LLP. (2024). Lipsky Lowe LLP. https://lipskylowe.com/services/wrongful-termination/covid-terminations/

Mello, M. M., & Parmet, W. E. (2023, September 7). Accommodating Religious Objections to Vaccination Mandates—Implications of Groff v DeJoy for Health Care Employers. JAMA Health Forum. https://doi.org/10.1001/jamahealthforum.2023.3672

Ong, F. W. (2024, August 28). A Religious Accommodation Claim May Be Based, in Part, on Non-Religious Terms. - Shawe Rosenthal LLP. Shawe Rosenthal LLP. https://shawe.com/eupdate/a-religious-accommodation-claim-may-be-based-in-part-on-non-religious-terms/

Will Ending Vaccine Mandates Expose Employers to Lawsuits? | WorldatWork. (2023). Worldatwork.org; WorldatWork. https://worldatwork.org/workspan/articles/will-ending-vaccine-mandates-expose-employers-to-lawsuits-

Part II: The Evidence Against the COVID Vaccine That Employers Ignored

Chapter 3 What Robert F. Kennedy Jr. Revealed About the Vaccine's Dangers

Robert F. Kennedy Jr.'s revelations about vaccine dangers have sparked significant debate and curiosity across various circles, from health professionals to legal experts. As vaccines remain a staple in public health strategy, understanding the full scope of their implications requires a closer look at the narratives presented by advocates like Kennedy. While vaccines are celebrated for their role in combating infectious diseases, it's essential to balance this narrative with a comprehensive examination of potential risks and controversies that unfold. Delving into these complex dynamics is crucial for anyone seeking a nuanced understanding of current vaccine discourse.

This chapter explores the multi-layered concerns surrounding vaccine safety and legal protections offered to pharmaceutical companies. It addresses how transparency issues and strategic communication may obscure critical safety data, raising questions about scientific integrity. The discussion extends to real-world consequences, examining cases of myocarditis and thrombotic events linked to vaccines, as well as the role of non-disclosure agreements in stifling open dialogue. Furthermore, it probes into the legal frameworks that shield manufacturers from liability, questioning their impact on accountability and consumer protection. Through an investigative lens, this chapter aims to equip readers with insights into ongoing debates, the balance between innovation and safety, and the possible legal repercussions stemming from these contentious revelations.

Transparency and Cover-Ups

An exploration into how vaccine injury data has been obscured reveals a landscape rife with historical examples where critical information was omitted from public view. One notable case is the controversy surrounding the MMR (Measles-Mumps-Rubella) vaccine, where Dr. William Thompson, a senior scientist at the CDC, claimed that data linking the vaccine to autism-like symptoms in African American boys was intentionally excluded from a study published in 2004 (Hooker, 2014). The implications of such omissions extend beyond public health debates, impacting trust in scientific integrity and transparency.

Methods to limit access to crucial safety information often involve strategic communication tactics and selective reporting. During the development and rollout of COVID-19 vaccines, some critics argued that adverse events were under-reported in official channels or framed in ways that minimized perceived risks. These concerns were accentuated by reports of myocarditis and blood clotting following vaccination, which led regulatory bodies like the FDA and CDC to briefly suspend the Johnson & Johnson vaccine until further notice (McNamara, 2021). Such actions highlight the delicate balance between maintaining public confidence in vaccine programs and ensuring complete transparency about potential adverse effects.

Moreover, non-disclosure agreements (NDAs) play a significant role in restricting information sharing among health professionals. In several high-profile cases, pharmaceutical companies have required healthcare workers and involved researchers to sign NDAs, effectively muzzling them from speaking about their findings or experiences related to vaccine injuries. This practice curtails open scientific discourse and hampers the flow of information necessary for evaluating vaccine safety comprehensively.

Regulatory bodies, intended as watchdogs, have sometimes been implicated in censoring adverse effect data. Critics have accused these organizations of having conflicts of interest due to close relationships with pharmaceutical companies they regulate. In one example, emails released through freedom of information requests showed conversations between FDA officials and Pfizer representatives discussing the timing and narrative of clinical trial data releases, raising questions about the impartiality of drug approval processes ("- FOLLOW the SCIENCE?: OVERSIGHT of the BIDEN COVID-19 ADMINISTRATIVE STATE RESPONSE", 2024).

In parallel, the impact of censorship extends to shaping public perception and policy direction. When dissenting voices are silenced or labeled as "anti-vaxxers," it creates an environment where only consensus opinions are heard, stifling innovation and adaptation in response to new evidence. This atmosphere is compounded by media portrayals that often dismiss or ridicule vaccine skeptics, thereby alienating groups who might otherwise contribute constructively to discussions on vaccine safety (Elisha et al., 2022).

The culmination of these practices results in a complex tapestry of power dynamics and ethical considerations, underscoring the necessity for vigilance and advocacy in ensuring transparency. While regulation is essential for safeguarding public health, it is equally crucial to guard against overreach that stifles legitimate scrutiny. Navigating this terrain requires ongoing dialogue between regulators, scientists, and the public, facilitated by transparency and ethical engagement rather than coercive silence.

Addressing these challenges involves acknowledging past oversights and implementing measures that promote openness. Initiatives could include revising disclosure requirements to make all clinical trial data publicly available and fostering independent oversight committees free from industry influence. Furthermore, encouraging a culture of transparency within regulatory bodies can help restore public trust and enable more informed decision-making regarding vaccine utilization and risk assessment.

Increased Risk of Health Complications

In recent years, vaccines have been heralded as a cornerstone of public health, yet some voices raise pressing concerns regarding their safety. Robert F. Kennedy Jr.'s revelations about vaccine dangers invite scrutiny into these claims. A primary area of concern is the incidence of myocarditis post-vaccination, particularly following COVID-19 vaccinations. Myocarditis, an inflammation of the heart muscle, has garnered attention due to reported cases post-vaccine administration. According to data analyzed from Vaccine Adverse Event Reporting Systems (VAERS), a distinct uptick in myocarditis cases, especially among young males aged 15-17, has been observed after receiving COVID-19 vaccines (Heidecker et al., 2022). Despite being rare, the occurrence is significant enough to prompt investigations into potential causal links between vaccines and this condition.

Furthermore, examining the correlation between vaccination and blood clot occurrences is crucial. The advent of COVID-19 vaccines, particularly those leveraging adenoviral vectors, brought forth reports of thrombotic events, leading to conditions such as vaccine-induced immune thrombotic thrombocytopenia (VITT) (Mahroum et al., 2022). The implications of these findings emphasize the need for more research into the pathophysiological mechanisms triggering such reactions. Blood clots can lead to severe health outcomes if not promptly addressed, making it vital to understand the potential risks associated with immunization processes.

Another aspect demanding attention is the connection between vaccines and autoimmune disorders. The rapid development and deployment of COVID-19 vaccines utilized novel technologies, primarily mRNA-based platforms, which stirred debates about their long-term safety. Conditions such as Guillain-Barre syndrome and transverse myelitis have been studied for any association with vaccines, drawing on past vaccine data to discern trends (Mahroum et al., 2022). Although definitive causal relationships remain elusive due to their rarity, ongoing monitoring and reporting are indispensable to mitigate these risks and assuage public fears.

Discrepancies between clinical trials and real-world outcomes further fuel the debate over vaccine safety. During controlled trials, vaccines displayed high efficacy rates with minimal adverse effects. However, the broader application revealed unexpected side effects that were not apparent during smaller-scale studies. For instance, the widespread use of certain vaccines highlighted concerns like myocarditis, more predominant in real-world settings than initially reported. This gap underscores the importance of robust post-marketing surveillance systems to capture comprehensive safety profiles over time.

Moreover, a key observation is how real-world data collection helps balance safety assertions made during clinical trials. The passive nature of many reporting systems means actual incident rates could be higher than current data suggest, emphasizing the need for active surveillance and thorough investigation to refine understanding (Heidecker et al., 2022). By comparing clinical trial stages to real-world applications, researchers can better identify patterns that may predict adverse health outcomes, ultimately improving vaccine designs and rollout strategies.

While acknowledging the beneficial roles that vaccines play in controlling infectious diseases, it is imperative to critically analyze scientific evidence that challenges the unyielding narrative of vaccines being universally "safe and effective." Public trust hinges on transparent communication and rigorous scientific inquiry. Addressing uncertainties head-on builds credibility and empowers individuals with information necessary for informed decision-making.

Legal Protections for Vaccine Manufacturers

In discussing the complex landscape of vaccine liability, it's crucial to understand how major pharmaceutical companies have been shielded from legal repercussions. This immunity stems largely from a combination of legislation and strategic agreements aimed at protecting these corporations, while simultaneously raising questions about accountability in public safety.

The first layer of this protective framework is the legal statutes granting immunity to vaccine producers. In various jurisdictions, laws have been crafted to absolve manufacturers of liability for adverse effects caused by their vaccines. These legal frameworks often cite public health imperatives, arguing that shielding companies from lawsuits encourages innovation and ensures an uninterrupted supply of vaccines. However, such immunity raises concerns about consumer protection and the extent to which companies are incentivized to prioritize safety over speed. For instance, the 1986 National Childhood Vaccine Injury Act in the United States established a no-fault compensation program for vaccine injuries, effectively limiting the circumstances under which manufacturers could be held liable (Prevention, 1985).

Government indemnity agreements represent another pillar of immunity for pharmaceutical companies. During public health emergencies, governments may enter into contracts with vaccine producers, agreeing to cover any potential legal costs or damages arising from vaccine-related injuries. These agreements aim to expedite vaccine distribution during crises, but they also transfer the financial risk from corporations to taxpayers. The COVID-19 pandemic saw several governments around the world signing such indemnity agreements to ensure rapid deployment of vaccines (Review & Saj Sundar Sri-Kumar, 2023). While these measures are intended to mitigate risk for manufacturers, they can create a moral hazard if companies become less cautious about potential side effects.

Additionally, the financial influence of pharmaceutical companies on political decisions cannot be overlooked. Through lobbying and campaign contributions, these corporations exert significant pressure on policymakers. This influence often results in favorable legislation and regulatory decisions that protect corporate interests. Critics argue that this financial clout undermines democratic processes and compromises public health policy. The Global Health Security Agenda has highlighted the necessity for equitable liability regimes that balance the interests of developers and the public (Webinar on Promoting Legal Preparedness & Equity Through Liability Risk Management, 2022). Despite these calls for reform, the entrenchment of corporate influence remains a formidable barrier to change.

Case studies of lawsuits dismissed under liability protections further illustrate the challenges faced by individuals seeking redress for vaccine injuries. In many instances, claimants must navigate a convoluted legal system stacked against them. Judicial precedents often favor manufacturers, as courts interpret existing laws in ways that uphold corporate immunity. Notable cases include those involving adverse reactions to widely used vaccines, where plaintiffs struggle to prove negligence or causation due to the robust legal defenses available to defendants. The obstacles in pursuing these lawsuits underscore the difficulty of holding vaccine producers accountable within the current legal framework.

Despite the complexities surrounding liability protections, there is a growing call for reform. Advocates suggest implementing systems that strike a balance between encouraging vaccine development and ensuring accountability. Proposals include the establishment of independent review panels to assess vaccine safety, stricter oversight of manufacturer practices, and transparent communication of known risks to the public. Such measures seek to restore trust in vaccination programs while addressing legitimate concerns about safety and corporate responsibility.

Implications for Wrongful Termination Cases

In recent times, the debates surrounding vaccine mandates, particularly COVID-19 vaccines, have intensified. A critical perspective in this debate has been that of Robert F. Kennedy Jr., who has been vocal about the dangers associated with these mandates. His arguments have illuminated a broader discussion on employee rights and legal repercussions, highlighting why his findings cannot be ignored.

Firstly, understanding the legal framework surrounding employee rights and vaccine mandates is crucial for both workers and employers. At the heart of this issue lies the question of individual autonomy versus public health. Employers have faced substantial pressure to implement vaccine mandates, often under the assumption that it would ensure workplace safety and compliance with health regulations. However, as some experts argue, such mandates could conflict with existing employee rights protected by law. The Equal Employment Opportunity Commission (EEOC) has stated that while employers may encourage vaccinations, they must also provide accommodations for those unable to receive them due to medical reasons or sincerely held religious beliefs (Federal Government Says Employers Can Mandate COVID-19 Vaccines? Not so Fast..., 2021). This underscores the need for clear communication and flexibility in policy implementation to prevent legal challenges.

The role of documented vaccine risks in court cases further accentuates the complexity of these mandates. In several instances, individuals have brought lawsuits against employers for imposing mandatory vaccinations, citing adverse reactions as a primary concern. For instance, Jennifer Bridges and over 100 employees at Methodist Hospital in Texas filed a lawsuit challenging the hospital's vaccine mandate, arguing that it violated their right to refuse an Emergency Use Authorization (EUA) vaccine (Federal Government Says Employers Can Mandate COVID-19 Vaccines? Not so Fast..., 2021). Such legal battles highlight the significant weight that documented vaccine risks can have in judicial proceedings, potentially swaying outcomes in favor of employees when sufficient evidence is presented.

Adding to this is the mounting evidence from testimonies affirming coercion in workplace vaccination policies. Many employees have reported feeling pressured or coerced into receiving vaccinations, fearing job loss or punitive measures if they refused. These testimonies have been pivotal in legal discussions, providing firsthand accounts of the undue stress and duress experienced by workers. Legal analysts argue that this element of coercion could constitute a violation of labor laws, leading to potential grounds for wrongful termination claims. As discussed in relevant cases, forcing employees to choose between their jobs and personal health decisions can be seen as infringing upon their rights.

Why This Matters for Wrongful Termination Cases: Using RFK Jr.'s findings as evidence that vaccine mandates were unjustified may serve as a compelling argument in wrongful termination lawsuits. The lack of consensus on mandatory vaccination policies, combined with the potential health risks highlighted by RFK Jr., could bolster claims of unjust treatment by employers. Employees terminated for non-compliance may find a potent ally in these findings, strengthening their position in court by questioning the legality and necessity of such mandates.

Lastly, exploring precedents set by successful wrongful termination claims provides insight into the evolving landscape of vaccine mandate litigation. Notable cases like Legaretta v. Fernando Macias in New Mexico, where an employee argued wrongful termination due to refusal of an EUA-status vaccine, illustrate emerging trends in legal rulings (Federal Government Says Employers Can Mandate COVID-19 Vaccines? Not so Fast..., 2021). These cases demonstrate a growing recognition of employee rights in the context of mandatory vaccinations, paving the way for future legal interpretations.

Insights and Implications

The chapter delves into the thorny issue of vaccine safety and the legal ramifications that come with it. We've explored how transparency, or the lack thereof, impacts public trust in vaccines. Key cases, from the MMR controversy to COVID-19 challenges, underline the complexities behind the data we rely on for making informed decisions. These discussions are crucial for anyone facing consequences due to vaccine disagreements, like wrongfully terminated employees or healthcare workers caught in policy crossfires. By understanding these dynamics, readers are better prepared to navigate their own battles against mandates they believe overstep personal freedoms.

Turning to the legal landscape, the chapter sheds light on how protective laws shield vaccine manufacturers, leaving individuals with limited recourse. We see how this plays out in the courtroom, where proving vaccine-related claims is often an uphill battle thanks to existing protections for pharmaceutical companies. Yet, as more people question these frameworks and seek justice for wrongful terminations, there is a growing call for reform. The pressing need for transparency and accountability resonates with those who champion medical freedom and highlights the importance of advocating for change in policies that affect us all.

Reference List

"Because I Said So: Examining the Science and Impact of COVID-19 Vaccine Mandates." (2025). Congress.gov. https://www.congress.gov/event/118th-congress/house-event/116287/text

Elisha, E., Guetzkow, J., Shir-Raz, Y., & Ronel, N. (2022, May 19). Suppressing Scientific Discourse on Vaccines? Self-perceptions of researchers and practitioners. HEC Forum. https://doi.org/10.1007/s10730-022-09479-7

- FOLLOW THE SCIENCE?: OVERSIGHT OF THE BIDEN COVID-19 ADMINISTRATIVE STATE RESPONSE. (2024). Govinfo.gov. https://www.govinfo.gov/content/pkg/CHRG-118hhrg56175/html/CHRG-118hhrg56175.htm

Federal Government Says Employers Can Mandate COVID-19 Vaccines? Not So Fast.... (2021). Brownstein Hyatt Farber Schreck. https://www.bhfs.com/insights/alerts-articles/2021/federal-government-says-employers-can-mandate-covid-19-vaccines-not-so-fast

Heidecker, B., Dagan, N., Balicer, R., Eriksson, U., Rosano, G., Coats, A., Tschöpe, C., Kelle, S., Poland, G. A., Frustaci, A., Klingel, K., Martin, P., Hare, J. M., Cooper, L. T., Pantazis, A., Imazio, M., Prasad, S., & Lüscher, T. F. (2022, October 6). Myocarditis following COVID-19 vaccine: Incidence, presentation, diagnosis, pathophysiology, therapy, and outcomes put into perspective. A clinical consensus document supported by the heart failure association of the european society of cardiology (ESC) and the ESC working group on myocardial and pericardial diseases. European Journal of Heart Failure. https://doi.org/10.1002/ejhf.2669

Mahroum, N., Lavine, N., Ohayon, A., Seida, R., Alwani, A., Alrais, M., Zoubi, M., & Bragazzi, N. L. (2022, July 5). COVID-19 Vaccination and the Rate of Immune and Autoimmune Adverse Events Following Immunization: Insights From a Narrative Literature Review. Frontiers in Immunology. https://doi.org/10.3389/fimmu.2022.872683

Prevention, N. R. C. (US) D. of H. P. and D. (1985). Liability for the Production and Sale of Vaccines. Www.ncbi.nlm.nih.gov; National Academies Press (US). https://www.ncbi.nlm.nih.gov/books/NBK216813/

Review, S. L., & Saj Sundar Sri-Kumar. (2023, December 2). Stanford Law Review. Stanford Law Review. https://www.stanfordlawreview.org/online/long-term-immunity-protecting-drug-developers-from-liability-for-late-occurring-serious-reactions-to-emergency-vaccines/

Chapter 4 Adverse Effects and Growing Legal Challenges Against Vaccine Mandates

Vaccine mandates have sparked fierce debates and legal challenges across various sectors, reshaping policies and practices in unprecedented ways. As institutions grapple with this evolving landscape, the complexities of enforcing such mandates become glaringly apparent, particularly when their implications reach into areas as vital as military readiness, healthcare, and workplace dynamics. The introduction of these mandates has not only stirred controversy but also brought to light significant concerns about individual freedoms and bodily autonomy. Critics argue that the measure has led to wrongful terminations and a sense of coercion, impacting thousands of individuals from diverse professional backgrounds.

In this chapter, we delve into the multifaceted legal battles surrounding vaccine mandates, examining the intricacies of executive orders and their ramifications for the balance of power between federal and state jurisdictions. The narrative unfolds through the experiences of military personnel dismissed for non-compliance, highlighting the tension between national security imperatives and personal choice. We further explore the critical role of medical whistleblowers who expose the ethical dilemmas faced by healthcare workers caught in the crossfire of mandate enforcement. By dissecting institutional responses, including modifications to health protocols and shifts in employee relations, this chapter provides a comprehensive overview of how organizations are navigating legal challenges. Whether you're seeking insights on potential policy shifts or understanding the broader societal impact, this section offers an in-depth look at the dynamic interplay between public health objectives and individual rights.

Military Personnel Dismissals and Reinstatements

In recent years, the military faced a significant upheaval as thousands of service members were dismissed for refusing the COVID-19 vaccine. From August 2021 to January 2023, under the Biden administration, more than 8,000 troops were discharged because they did not comply with the mandate requiring vaccination against COVID-19. This accounted for less than 1% of the total military, yet it sparked considerable controversy and became a focal point for political debates and legal battles. The primary reasons cited by those who refused the vaccine included religious objections and personal beliefs about bodily autonomy. Despite the small percentage, the dismissals were used by critics to argue that such measures could potentially undermine military readiness and morale, casting doubt on the administration's policies (Weixel, 2025).

A pivotal development came with President Trump's executive order in 2025, which called for the reinstatement of these service members with full back pay and benefits. This move was consistent with his previous campaign promises and marked a shift in the administration's stance toward the mandates. Defense Secretary Pete Hegseth confirmed during his confirmation hearing that this step would include an apology to affected service members, further enhancing the appeal of returning to active duty (Weixel, 2025). The executive order from President Trump aimed not only to rectify what many viewed as wrongful terminations but also to bolster the military ranks by encouraging former service members to reintegrate.

One crucial aspect of Trump's executive order is its provision for back pay and benefits for those opting for reinstatement. However, the order also leaves several questions unanswered. While it outlines the promise of back pay, it does not specify any conditions or additional service obligations associated with this benefit. Furthermore, there is no clear method described for funding the potential increase in salaries if thousands of troops are reinstated (Konstantin Toropin, 2025). This has led to some confusion and concern among both military personnel and policymakers regarding the feasibility and implementation of the order.

For civilian employees in similar positions, Trump's executive order could set a precedent. Although the order directly addresses military personnel, its implications extend to civilian workers terminated under comparable circumstances. If military members can be reinstated with full benefits, a similar argument could be made for civilians seeking justice after losing their jobs for refusing vaccinations. This raises significant legal questions and may prompt reevaluations of existing policies across various sectors, where litigation and advocacy have already been active (Konstantin Toropin, 2025).

The reinstatement process itself, while presenting an opportunity for affected service members, poses challenges both administratively and operationally. Only a small fraction of the discharged troops have returned to service since the vaccine mandate rescindment in 2023. As data indicates, although over 8,000 service members were separated, a mere 43 chose to reapply initially, and by 2025 just 113 had returned to military service, including 73 soldiers, 25 Marines, 13 airmen or Guardians, and two sailors (Konstantin Toropin, 2025). This hesitancy can largely be attributed to uncertainties surrounding the terms of reinstatement and the assurance of back pay.

The broader impact of these policies on military morale and operational readiness cannot be underestimated. The dismissal of thousands of service members undoubtedly reshaped the dynamics within the military, with units having to adjust to sudden changes in personnel. The reinstatement, while potentially beneficial in restoring numbers, requires careful management to ensure that morale is not adversely affected by the perceived flip-flop in policy. Additionally, integrating returning service members smoothly into their roles necessitates thoughtful planning and support to maintain cohesive unit cohesion and effectiveness.

Guidelines concerning the executive order are necessary to navigate these complexities successfully. Firstly, it is essential to clearly communicate the terms of reinstatement to all eligible service members. It should include detailed explanations of back pay provisions, rank restoration, and any associated service commitments. Secondly, providing counseling and reintegration programs can help returning troops acclimate to the current military environment, addressing any sense of dislocation or apprehension. Lastly, transparent communication within the military hierarchy and between governmental bodies is crucial to manage expectations and ensure a smooth implementation of the order.

Executive Orders and Their Legal Ramifications

In the discourse surrounding vaccine mandates, executive orders have emerged as pivotal instruments wielded by authorities to enforce public health directives. Understanding their legal authority and limitations is crucial for comprehending their broader implications. Executive orders in the realm of public health are generally issued by a president or governor to address urgent issues requiring immediate action. They derive their authority from statutory laws that delegate specific powers to executive branches, enabling them to enforce regulations swiftly without going through legislative processes. However, these orders must align with the constitutional framework and cannot overstep the bounds set by existing laws.

A key limitation of executive orders lies in their temporary nature and susceptibility to judicial review. Courts can invalidate these orders if they exceed the authority granted or infringe upon individual rights as protected by the Constitution. For instance, if an order is deemed to violate the principle of separation of powers or encroach on states' rights, it may be struck down. The contours of their legality often attract rigorous scrutiny, especially when they intersect with complex domains like healthcare and individual freedoms.

The influence of executive orders on the balance of power between federal and state jurisdictions presents another layer of complexity. In the United States, public health traditionally falls under state jurisdiction. However, federal executive orders can exert pressure on states to comply with national standards, especially when tied to federal funding. This dynamic can create tension, as seen when states resist perceived federal overreach. When federal mandates compel state action, they may be contested in courtrooms, often resulting in landmark rulings that redefine jurisdictional boundaries.

Precedent-setting cases in this context serve as barometers for understanding the reach and limits of executive orders. For example, the recent Supreme Court decision to block the Occupational Safety and Health Administration (OSHA) mandate highlights the court's role in delineating the scope of federal agency power. OSHA's rule mandating vaccination or weekly testing for large companies was invalidated because it exceeded the agency's statutory authority, according to the majority opinion. Conversely, the Centers for Medicare and Medicaid Services (CMS) mandate for healthcare workers was upheld, as it fell within the agency's regulatory purview (School, 2022).

Such decisions illustrate the nuanced interpretations courts apply, often hinging on the specificity of delegated powers and the context of agency action. These rulings underscore the significance of crafting narrowly tailored executive orders with clear statutory backing to withstand legal scrutiny.

Moreover, the evolving landscape of judicial opinions on vaccine mandates inevitably prompts considerations for legislative or policy changes. Judicial outcomes not only offer clarity but also propel policymakers to re-evaluate existing laws. If courts signal that current statutes are inadequate for addressing public health challenges, it could lead to legislative reforms aimed at fortifying the legal foundation for future executive actions.

For instance, if a particular judicial decision exposes gaps in statutory guidance, Congress or state legislatures might respond by drafting more explicit laws detailing the permissible scope of executive authority in crises. This preemptive legislative action can mitigate the uncertainty associated with relying solely on executive orders during health emergencies (Staff, 2022).

Guidance for stakeholders navigating this complex legal terrain includes closely monitoring litigation trends and adapting policies accordingly. Organizations facing mandates should prepare for potential legal challenges by ensuring compliance aligns with both federal and state regulations. Inclusion of legal experts in policy formulation can help anticipate judicial reactions and fortify defense strategies against possible lawsuits.

Medical Whistleblowers and Legal Battles

Healthcare professionals have emerged as pivotal figures in illuminating the contentious issues surrounding vaccine mandate enforcement. Many medical staff have courageously voiced concerns about these mandates, often facing significant risks to their careers and personal lives. Their testimonies provide invaluable insights into the complexities of mandate-related misconduct.

Several healthcare workers have stepped forward with firsthand accounts of how vaccine mandates were implemented in ways they deemed unethical or coercive. These testimonies reveal a troubling pattern of institutional pressure and retaliation against those who dared to question the prevailing policies. For example, some medical professionals reported being threatened with job loss or professional censure if they refused the vaccine, despite having legitimate health concerns or religious objections. Such accounts underscore the perceived lack of transparency and fairness in how some institutions handled exemption requests. A key source that highlights these issues states, "Health care workers have been fired, faced new restrictions, and even been detained for voicing their safety concerns" (Silenced and Endangered: Clinicians' Human Rights and Health Concerns about Their Facilities' Response to COVID-19, n.d.).

In response to these unilateral decisions, numerous lawsuits have been filed against institutions accused of dismissing valid exemption requests. These legal actions argue that the denial of exemptions, whether for medical or religious reasons, often lacked a sound scientific basis and violated individuals' rights to bodily autonomy. In many cases, plaintiffs assert that institutions acted punitively without considering the specific circumstances of each exemption request. The nature of these lawsuits is indicative of a wider backlash against what is perceived as overreach by organizations prioritizing compliance over individual rights. According to Bardosh et al. (2022), there are ongoing societal debates about whether "current vaccine policies, rather than being science-based, are being driven by sociopolitical attitudes."

Whistleblowers play a critical role in exposing such alleged misconduct but face a precarious situation fraught with risks. Those who have publicly criticized mandate enforcement have often encountered significant professional repercussions, including threats to their employment and reputational damage. The climate created by these repercussions can be chilling, deterring others from speaking out and stifling essential discourse on public health and safety. However, whistleblower protections exist to shield these individuals from retaliation, yet their effectiveness varies across jurisdictions and institutions. In the report by Physicians for Human Rights, it is noted that healthcare workers "faced reprisals and retaliation worldwide... for speaking out in defense of the safety and rights of patients and health care workers," which exemplifies the risks involved in coming forward (Silenced and Endangered: Clinicians' Human Rights and Health Concerns about Their Facilities' Response to COVID-19, n.d.).

The influence of legal actions instigated by healthcare professionals has profound implications for hospital policy and public trust. As these cases unfold, hospital administrators are increasingly compelled to reconsider their policies regarding vaccine mandates. Legal outcomes could drive changes towards more balanced approaches that consider both public health priorities and individual rights. Additionally, the public scrutiny associated with high-profile lawsuits can intensify pressure on institutions to enhance transparency and accountability in decision-making processes.

Moreover, the public perception of healthcare institutions is at stake. As reports of lawsuits and whistleblower disclosures garner media attention, they contribute to shaping public opinion about the integrity of healthcare systems. Trust in these institutions hinges on their ability to demonstrate fairness and adherence to ethical standards, particularly amid a pandemic where public cooperation is vital.

As the landscape continues to shift, the experiences and legal battles faced by healthcare professionals reveal broader systemic challenges within the implementation of vaccine mandates. They highlight the necessity for clear, consistent guidelines that respect both public health objectives and individual liberties. Moving forward, institutions may need to engage more proactively with their employees to foster an environment where diverse perspectives on public health measures can coexist without fear of reprisal.

Institutional Responses and Policy Shifts

As institutions face mounting legal challenges against vaccine mandates, adapting to this evolving landscape has become imperative. Organizations across various sectors are employing a range of strategies to address these challenges, resulting in significant changes to their policies and practices.

A primary strategy involves active engagement with legal experts to navigate the intricate web of regulations and court rulings impacting vaccine mandates. Institutions are increasingly relying on legal consultants to assess compliance risks and develop robust legal defenses. This approach not only ensures adherence to current laws but also prepares organizations for potential litigation. Some companies have established dedicated task forces or committees focused on monitoring legal developments and shaping responsive policies.

Another crucial adaptation involves modifying health and safety protocols in response to court decisions. Recent rulings have prompted major corporations to reassess their stance on mandatory vaccination policies. For instance, some companies have shifted from strict mandates to more flexible approaches, such as encouraging vaccinations while providing regular testing as an alternative. This shift often aims to strike a balance between employee rights and workplace safety, demonstrating how legal outcomes can drive institutional policy evolution.

The impact of court rulings is also evident in changes to employee relations and human resources practices related to health mandates. Organizations are revising their communication strategies to emphasize transparency and foster trust among employees. Clear and consistent messaging about health requirements and available accommodations has become essential. Moreover, HR departments are now more involved in developing exemption processes and ensuring that they are applied fairly and consistently, in line with legal guidelines.

HR practices are also undergoing transformation as companies strive to maintain employee morale amid contentious mandate debates. Employee resource groups and wellness programs are being leveraged to provide support and address concerns related to health mandates. By promoting dialogue and offering assistance, organizations can create an inclusive environment that mitigates polarization and supports mental well-being.

Looking ahead, ongoing legal developments will likely continue to influence institutional policies. Predictions for future adaptations include increased flexibility in workplace arrangements, with hybrid work models becoming more prevalent. Organizations might also invest more in digital infrastructure to support remote operations, reducing reliance on traditional office settings. These shifts aim to accommodate diverse employee needs while mitigating legal risks associated with mandates.

Furthermore, future policies could prioritize individual choice by expanding exemptions and accommodating personal health beliefs, provided they do not compromise public health goals. Companies may explore innovative ways to incentivize vaccinations, such as through wellness programs or financial rewards, rather than enforcing strict mandates.

To ensure long-term resilience, institutions must remain agile in their legal strategy, continuously updating policies to reflect the latest regulatory changes and court interpretations. Engaging with policymakers and contributing to public discourse on vaccine mandates can also position organizations as proactive leaders in shaping health policy frameworks.

Insights and Implications

The chapter has delved into the intricate web of legal and institutional responses to vaccine mandates, particularly focusing on military, medical, and broader organizational contexts. We've explored how military personnel dismissals have sparked significant debates and led to policy reversals, like President Trump's executive order for reinstatement. This move, while attempting to rectify perceived injustices, comes with its own set of challenges, including questions about funding and implementation. In parallel, we've seen how civilian sectors grapple with similar issues, as the policies guiding military reinstatements hold potential precedent-setting implications for civilian employees facing comparable situations.

Moreover, the impact of legal actions, especially those spurred by healthcare professionals and whistleblowers, underscores the ongoing tension between public health measures and individual rights. As these legal battles unfold, they are driving institutional shifts towards more transparent and flexible policies. Companies and institutions are increasingly relying on legal expertise to navigate compliance and reformulate strategies that balance safety with employee autonomy. This evolving landscape highlights the importance of maintaining open dialogue and adaptability as organizations strive to meet both legal obligations and ethical responsibilities. The culmination of these developments signals a shift towards more nuanced and inclusive approaches to handling mandates, encouraging a future where freedom and safety coexist without compromise.

Reference List

Bardosh, K., Figueiredo, A. de, Gur-Arie, R., Jamrozik, E., Doidge, J., Lemmens, T., Keshavjee, S., Graham, J. E., & Baral, S. (2022, May 25). The unintended consequences of COVID-19 vaccine policy: why mandates, passports and restrictions may cause more harm than good. BMJ Global Health. https://doi.org/10.1136/bmjgh-2022-008684

HR Resources for COVID-19 | USC Center for Effective Organizations. (n.d.). https://ceo.usc.edu/2023/02/08/coronavirus-2/

Konstantin Toropin. (2025, January 28). Trump Order on Back Pay for Vaccine Refusers Raises Questions, Offers No Clear Path Forward. Military.com. https://www.military.com/daily-news/2025/01/28/trump-order-back-pay-vaccine-refusers-raises-questions-offers-no-clear-path-forward.html

Navigating the Pathways of Vaccine Mandates and Current COVID-19 Litigation. (2021). SlideShare; Slideshare. https://www.slideshare.net/slideshow/navigating-the-pathways-of-vaccine-mandates-and-current-covid19-litigation/250853763

Silenced and Endangered: Clinicians' Human Rights and Health Concerns about Their Facilities' Response to COVID-19. (n.d.). PHR. https://phr.org/our-work/resources/silenced-and-endangered/

School, S. L. (2022, January 20). A Look at the Supreme Court Ruling on Vaccination Mandates. Stanford Law School. https://law.stanford.edu/2022/01/20/a-look-at-the-supreme-court-ruling-on-vaccination-mandates/

Staff, N. (2022, January 5). Federal Vaccine Mandates and Legal Challenges. NASHP. https://nashp.org/federal-vaccine-mandates-and-legal-challenges/

Weixel, N. (2025). Trump to reinstate military members dismissed for COVID-19 shot refusal. The Hill. Retrieved from https://thehill.com/policy/defense/5108499-trump-reinstatement-service-members-covid-vaccine/

Part III: Winning Court Battles Against Illegal Vaccine Mandates

Chapter 5 Wrongfully Fired, Rightfully Paid—Major Employee Wins

Wrongful termination cases often draw significant attention due to their complex nature and the profound impact they can have on both individual lives and corporate practices. At the heart of these disputes is usually a tension between employer policies and employee rights, a theme that resonates deeply with many who find themselves navigating similar challenges in today's job market. This chapter delves into some of the most high-profile cases where employees have successfully contested their dismissals in court, earning not just compensation but also setting important legal precedents. These stories are more than just legal victories; they offer lessons in resilience and serve as beacons for others facing similar battles.

In exploring these landmark cases, the chapter highlights key factors that contributed to the successful outcomes for the plaintiffs. Readers will gain insight into the intricacies of presenting strong evidence, the strategic importance of effective legal representation, and the invaluable role of thorough documentation in winning such cases. Moreover, it examines the wider implications of these legal victories for corporate policies, particularly how companies might reassess their protocols in light of costly penalties. Through real-life examples, this chapter offers a compelling look at how individuals can hold powerful entities accountable, inspiring hope and providing guidance for those seeking justice in the face of seemingly insurmountable odds.

The Michigan Blue Cross Blue Shield Lawsuit

In the world of employment, wrongful termination cases often serve as cautionary tales and benchmarks for justice. The case of Lisa Domski exemplifies the intricate legal journey to securing such justice, shedding light on the financial and ethical repercussions corporations face when found guilty of employee rights violations. Lisa Domski's story began with her termination from Blue Cross Blue Shield Michigan (BCBSM), following her refusal to comply with a company-mandated COVID-19 vaccination policy. Her unwavering stance, grounded in her religious beliefs, led to a lawsuit that not only vindicated her but also served as a significant financial blow to BCBSM, illustrating the heft of damages companies might incur when they fail to uphold their employees' rights.

Lisa Domski, an IT specialist with nearly four decades of service at BCBSM, faced dismissal after her request for a religious exemption from the company's vaccine requirement was denied. At the heart of her legal victory were several pivotal factors: the strength of the evidence she presented, the advocacy skills of her attorney, Jon Marko, and the federal jury's assessment of BCBSM's conduct. Domski had provided detailed documentation, including a written statement of her religious beliefs and contacts for her priest, which demonstrated her sincerity and compliance with the company's accommodation process. Her ability to work remotely since the pandemic began further questioned the necessity of the vaccine mandate for her specific role. According to the court, the failure of BCBSM to properly engage with these accommodations was a blatant violation of her religious rights, resulting in a substantial $12.7 million award. These damages consisted of $10 million in punitive damages, underscoring the jury's perception of malice in BCBSM's handling of Domski's request, alongside compensation for lost wages and noneconomic damages. Such an award showcases how costly it can be for companies to neglect or dismiss legitimate employee grievances.

The broader implications of this case extend beyond monetary figures. From a legal perspective, Lisa Domski's victory highlights the critical importance of thorough documentation and robust legal representation in navigating workplace disputes over mandates and personal convictions.

Successful outcomes in wrongful termination cases often depend on the clarity and consistency of evidence presented, as well as the expertise of legal counsel who can effectively argue breaches of employee rights. For employees in similar positions, Domski's triumph offers hope and a potential template for pursuing justice – emphasizing the real possibility of holding employers accountable in court.

Corporate entities, especially those enforcing widespread health mandates, must note the broader implications of Domski's case. In today's environment, where employee autonomy and company policies frequently clash, businesses are compelled to carefully balance safety protocols with respect for individual rights. Employers are obligated to ensure that policies allow for reasonable accommodations and protect against discrimination based on religious or personal beliefs. Failure to do so can result in more than just reputational harm; it can lead to crippling financial liabilities and set legal precedents that influence future policy-making.

As a reaction to Lisa Domski's case, companies like BCBSM may find themselves revisiting and revising their policies to prevent repeat scenarios. Corporate policies post-lawsuit are likely to become more nuanced, with procedures for exemptions and accommodations under tighter scrutiny. Legal departments will play a crucial role in crafting frameworks that align with both state and federal laws, ensuring decisions regarding employee health mandates are fair and respectful of diverse perspectives. Additionally, human resources professionals will need to facilitate open dialogues between management and staff, fostering an environment where concerns can be addressed proactively rather than reactively.

Ultimately, the ripple effects of Domski's case remind us that the stakes in wrongful termination suits are high and multifaceted. Businesses must recognize the essential duty they hold in respecting employee rights while implementing necessary safety measures. For employees and advocates, her story reinforces the ongoing struggle for equitable workplace treatment and the power of perseverance in challenging unjust practices. As corporate America moves forward, cases like Lisa Domski's will continue to shape the landscape of employment law, encouraging a culture of fairness and accountability across all sectors. The lessons learned here echo the broader conversation about the balance of power between employers and employees, urging each party to engage mindfully and ethically in their professional relationships.

The BART Transit Workers' Lawsuit

The transit workers' case presents a captivating exploration of the collision between employee autonomy and public health mandates. Six transit employees were awarded $1.3 million each after challenging vaccine mandates, marking one of the most significant legal victories in recent times regarding employment disputes over public health policies. This landmark case underscores the intricate balance required when enforcing workplace health mandates while respecting individual rights.

Public health requirements, especially in the wake of a global pandemic, have led to rigorous enforcement measures, often resulting in disputes over personal freedom versus collective safety. Such cases illuminate the broader implications for employee autonomy, as individuals are confronted with decisions that weigh personal beliefs against mandatory compliance for safety reasons. This particular case serves as a stark reminder of the challenges employers face in navigating these conflicts, highlighting the need for policies that respect both individual freedoms and community health standards.

Understandably, the role of unions and collective bargaining emerged as pivotal in this scenario. Unions, standing as the advocates for worker rights, played a crucial part by initiating the legal challenge and providing a platform for the grievances of the transit workers. Through collective bargaining, unions can negotiate terms that safeguard employee interests, ensuring that any mandate respects individual rights while meeting organizational needs. This advocacy was instrumental in achieving the settlement, demonstrating the power of organized labor in defending against what they perceived as unfair mandates.

From an employer's perspective, the need for carefully crafted health-related policies becomes evident. Implementing these policies demands sensitivity and adaptability, considering not only the legal aspects but also the ethical and psychological impacts on employees. Employers must navigate the fine line between ensuring workplace safety and infringing on personal autonomy. This case highlights the importance of engaging with employees and their representatives actively and openly to foster trust and mutual understanding, thereby reducing conflict potential.

Employers should consider several key factors when implementing health-related policies. First, policies must be transparent and communicated effectively to all stakeholders. It is essential to articulate the rationale behind mandates clearly, outlining the benefits of compliance and the repercussions of non-compliance. Secondly, offering alternatives or accommodations where possible can mitigate potential backlash. For instance, options such as remote work, regular testing, or unpaid leave for those unwilling to comply with vaccination mandates might be more palatable solutions.

Moreover, involving employees in policy formation through surveys or feedback sessions can help in creating more acceptable mandates. By incorporating employee perspectives, employers can develop balanced policies that protect public health without compromising personal liberties. This approach not only minimizes resistance but also fosters a sense of shared responsibility among the workforce.

The MGM Grand Detroit Lawsuit

In high-pressure environments like casinos, the implications of a wrongful termination case can ripple through the industry. Casinos are known for their volatile nature, characterized by fluctuating customer volumes and demanding operational conditions. These factors contribute to variable work environments that require adaptable employees and employers who uphold fair treatment and contractual obligations.

A landmark case involving a casino worker who successfully sued for $133,000 highlights this issue. This victory underscores the importance of adhering to fair treatment standards in industries with challenging work conditions. The employee's triumph serves as a critical reminder that all workers deserve respect and fair treatment, regardless of the industry's inherent unpredictability. For employees, it reinforces the belief that standing up against unfair labor practices is worth pursuing, even in environments where job security often feels uncertain.

The case hinged on the evidence leveraged by the employee, focusing primarily on contractual obligations that the employer failed to honor. In this instance, the employee was armed with detailed documentation of the agreements breached by the casino. These documents were pivotal in building a strong legal argument, proving that the worker's termination was indeed wrongful. Contractual obligations serve as the foundation of the employee-employer relationship; when these are violated, it not only affects the immediate parties involved but also sets a precedent for others within the sector.

From a broader perspective, the significance of maintaining robust human resources practices becomes evident, especially in industries like hospitality and gaming, where the stakes are high, and the pressure is relentless. Proper HR practices ensure that policies align with legal standards and protect both the interests of the organization and its employees. This is particularly vital in sectors where employee turnover is high, and work conditions can evolve rapidly. Implementing comprehensive training programs focused on labor laws and employee rights can help prevent similar cases in the future, fostering a more stable and legally compliant workplace environment.

Moreover, such legal victories can profoundly impact worker morale and company culture. When justice prevails in favor of wrongfully terminated employees, it sends a powerful message throughout the workforce: that justice can be achieved and that the organization values integrity and fairness. This can enhance morale among employees, knowing that their rights are safeguarded and that any grievances will be addressed seriously. Improved morale often translates into increased productivity and loyalty, contributing positively to the organizational culture.

Conversely, for the employer, losing a wrongful termination case can act as a catalyst for reassessment and change. It may prompt a review of corporate policies, encouraging management to implement changes that mitigate the risk of future litigation. Establishing clear communication channels between employees and management, alongside reinforcing trust through fair practices, becomes essential. Being proactive about inclusivity and fairness in HR practices can significantly improve relations across all levels of the business.

For other employees working under high pressure, the case serves as an influential blueprint of how to handle disputes over wrongful termination. It underscores the power of evidence-backed claims and the necessity of understanding one's employment rights. While high-pressure industries like hospitality and gaming might seem daunting due to their dynamic nature, this example shows that standing up for one's rights is possible and can lead to meaningful change.

What these developments mean for those navigating similar predicaments is crucial. Having access to legal support and understanding contractual rights are invaluable tools. Employees should feel empowered to voice concerns and seek legal guidance if they experience unfair treatment. It's a reminder of the importance of keeping thorough records of communications and agreements made with employers. By doing so, they strengthen their position in potential legal disputes.

Employees in similar sectors may take encouragement from this outcome, recognizing its relevance to their circumstances. With the knowledge that justice can be achieved, they can be better prepared to advocate for themselves in unfair situations. Such transparency and accountability are important steps toward more equitable workplaces where employees feel secure and valued.

Employers must take heed of these lessons by revisiting their employment practices to ensure compliance and fairness. It's about striking a balance between achieving business goals and respecting the workforce that helps realize those objectives. Reinforcing this balance with regular audits of HR policies and ongoing training can help build an environment where fairness reigns, reducing incidences of wrongful termination and enhancing overall morale and productivity.

The Educator's Fight Against Mandates

In recent years, the landscape of employment in education has shifted significantly, particularly with the imposition of various mandates that have led to complex legal battles. One notable triumph was a teacher's successful challenge against their dismissal, which not only set a precedent but also became a beacon for educators caught in similar predicaments. This case exemplifies how individual resolve can bring about systemic change within educational employment practices.

At the heart of this success story is the delicate balance between personal rights and institutional regulations. The educator in question leveraged legal strategies that underscored the importance of understanding one's rights in the face of institutional mandates. The crux of the argument lay in demonstrating how the mandate infringed on fundamental employment rights while navigating the intricacies of workplace policies. This approach served as an essential template for others contesting similar employment decisions.

The legal strategies employed in this case highlighted crucial aspects of employment law that are often overlooked by educators. By focusing on constitutional protections and contractual obligations, the teacher's legal team was able to build a robust defense. They emphasized the necessity for institutions to adhere strictly to due process and consider individual circumstances before enforcing blanket policies. This methodical dismantling of the institution's rationale for termination proved pivotal, revealing loopholes and misinterpretations of policy that favored the employee.

Furthermore, this case had ripple effects beyond the immediate legal victory. It prompted a reevaluation of mandate-related termination policies across different educational jurisdictions. School boards and administrative bodies were compelled to reassess their approaches, acknowledging the potential legal pitfalls of overly rigid enforcement. This shift in perspective not only helped safeguard the rights of educators but also influenced policymaking at higher levels, encouraging a more nuanced consideration of employment law implications when drafting such mandates.

For other educators facing mandates that threaten their job security, this case offers valuable lessons. It underscores the significance of being well-versed in both personal rights and institutional obligations. Educators are encouraged to seek clarity regarding their contracts, understand the scope of their legal protections, and engage with professional organizations or legal advisors when uncertainties arise. Knowledge of these legal frameworks can empower teachers to negotiate terms or challenge unfair dismissals confidently.

Moreover, this victory highlights the broader conversation about employment rights within the educational sector. By successfully challenging their dismissal, the teacher not only safeguarded their position but also initiated a dialogue about the role of mandates in educational administration. This discourse is instrumental in shaping future policies that respect employee autonomy while balancing institutional needs.

Educators can draw several practical lessons from this case. First, maintaining detailed records of communications and policy changes can be invaluable during legal proceedings. Such documentation provides concrete evidence that can bolster a case against wrongful termination. Second, aligning with colleagues and forming support networks can enhance collective bargaining power and provide moral support during challenging times.

Another aspect worth noting is the evolving nature of educational policy-making in response to such legal victories. As schools and districts become more aware of the legal challenges associated with mandates, there is a growing trend towards incorporating more flexible and inclusive policies. Decision-makers are beginning to recognize the value of engaging educators in policy discussions, ensuring that their voices are heard and considered in administrative processes.

This shift towards inclusivity not only benefits employees but also contributes positively to the overall educational environment. A workforce that feels valued and protected is more likely to be motivated and engaged, ultimately enhancing the quality of education students receive. Thus, the triumph of one educator extends its impact to the wider academic community, fostering an atmosphere where rights and responsibilities coexist harmoniously.

The case also serves as a reminder of the dynamic interplay between law and education. As legal precedents continue to influence educational policy, it becomes imperative for educators to stay informed about developments in employment law. Engaging with legal experts and professional organizations can provide ongoing insights into these evolving landscapes, equipping educators with the tools needed to navigate future challenges effectively.

Insights and Implications

The cases of wrongful termination explored in this chapter highlight the delicate balance between enforcing health-related mandates and respecting individual rights. Whether it's Lisa Domski's triumph against Blue Cross Blue Shield Michigan or the transit workers' substantial settlement, these stories illustrate how vital it is for employees to document their grievances thoroughly and seek competent legal counsel. Each case serves as a powerful example of how individuals can challenge corporate policies perceived as unjust, setting legal precedents that may influence future employment practices significantly. They remind us of the importance of personal conviction and the role legal victories play in reshaping workplace policies to accommodate diverse perspectives while ensuring fairness.

For businesses, these stories are cautionary tales emphasizing the potential repercussions of neglecting employee rights. The significant financial liabilities faced by companies like BCBSM underscore the necessity for employers to balance safety protocols with respect for personal beliefs. Employers must engage in open dialogue with their workforce, considering accommodations and respecting individual differences to avoid costly disputes. As these cases demonstrate, creating an environment where employee rights are upheld not only avoids litigation but also fosters a culture of trust and respect. This is crucial in maintaining productivity and morale, ultimately benefiting both the employees and the organization as a whole.

Reference List

Hunter, A. (2024, December 29). Top Labour Arbitration Cases of 2024 - Hunter Legal LLP. Hunter Legal LLP. https://hunterlegal.ca/top-labour-arbitration-cases-of-2024/

Hospitality. (2018, April 19). Littler Mendelson P.C. https://www.littler.com/hospitality

Izabel Modano. (2024, November 12). Catholic Woman Awarded Over $12 Million After Termination for Refusing COVID Vaccine. Lawyer Monthly. https://www.lawyer-monthly.com/2024/11/catholic-woman-awarded-over-12-million-after-termination-for-refusing-covid-vaccine/

Lawsuit Challenges COVID-19 Vaccine Mandate for Federal Prisons Employees. (n.d.). Government Executive. https://www.govexec.com/management/2021/10/lawsuit-challenges-covid-19-vaccine-mandate-federal-prisons-employees/186509/

MSN. (2025). Msn.com. https://www.msn.com/en-gb/health/health-news/catholic-woman-fired-for-refusing-covid-vaccine-wins-over-12m/ar-AA1tXrFe?ocid=sw

Notable Board Decisions | National Labor Relations Board. (2012). Nlrb.gov. https://www.nlrb.gov/cases-decisions/decisions/notable-board-decisions

Wells, M., & Clayton, C. (2019). Chapter 5: Ethical & Legal Issues in Education. Viva.pressbooks.pub. https://viva.pressbooks.pub/foundationsofamericaneducation/chapter/chapter-5/

hlr. (2015, January 12). Education Policy Litigation as Devolution. Harvard Law Review. https://harvardlawreview.org/print/vol-128/education-policy-litigation-as-devolution/

Chapter 6 Lawsuits Beyond Religious Exemptions

Examining lawsuits beyond religious exemptions dives into a labyrinth of legal complexities where personal rights and public health concerns collide. Employees who oppose mandatory vaccinations often find themselves navigating a challenging landscape where individual choice is pitted against workplace policies designed to safeguard collective health. This chapter explores the intricate world of legal battles that arise when employees challenge vaccine mandates, not on religious grounds but through various other avenues available under the law. These cases underline the broader debate over control and autonomy in medical decisions while highlighting the potential ramifications for workers across diverse fields.

Legal challenges against vaccine mandates extend beyond just religious exemptions and delve into areas like employment contract violations, discrimination claims under the Americans with Disabilities Act (ADA), and concerns about unsafe medical interventions. The chapter unpacks how employees leverage contractual terms to argue infringement on their health choices, reflecting deeper tensions between agreed-upon work conditions and evolving public health requirements. It examines ADA-based claims, where employees with medical conditions seek accommodations beyond a one-size-fits-all mandate approach. Furthermore, it scrutinizes allegations of enforcement of potentially unsafe medical practices by employers, exploring the balancing act between ensuring safety and risking liability from adverse reactions. Through these narratives, readers gain insights into the complex interplay between policy enforcement and individual rights, revealing the multifaceted nature of this ongoing debate.

Employees' Safety Concerns

In recent years, concerns about vaccine safety have emerged as a significant factor for employees opposing mandatory vaccination policies. These concerns often revolve around personal safety and the desire to maintain medical autonomy in health-related decisions.

Employees frequently cite potential side effects and the absence of long-term studies when expressing their apprehension about vaccines, particularly those developed rapidly, such as COVID-19 vaccines. There is a widespread perception that the speed of development may compromise thorough testing, leading to unknown future consequences. Such fears are not entirely unfounded, as new vaccines can, in rare instances, cause adverse effects that weren't evident during trials. Regulatory bodies like the CDC and the European Medicines Agency (EMA) actively monitor and report on these adverse events through systems like the EudraVigilance database, ensuring transparency and ongoing safety evaluations. However, this doesn't fully alleviate apprehensions, especially when sensationalized stories circulate on social media, amplifying skepticism (Goje & Kapoor, 2024).

Medical autonomy plays a crucial role in the debate surrounding mandatory vaccinations. Many employees feel their right to make individual health decisions is compromised by external mandates. This notion underscores the importance of self-determination in healthcare choices—an individual's ability to weigh risks and benefits and decide what's best without interference. Respect for medical autonomy aligns with the broader principle of informed consent, foundational to ethical medical practice. Employers imposing vaccination requirements sometimes seem incompatible with this principle, leading to legal challenges and tension between personal freedoms and public health objectives.

Misinformation has significantly contributed to shaping employee perceptions about vaccine safety. Often, misinformation spreads through social networks, peer discussions, and media, influencing perceptions and fueling hesitancy. During the COVID-19 pandemic, conflicting messages from different stakeholders and rapid developments in scientific understanding created a fertile ground for misunderstandings (Chirico & Teixeira da

Silva, 2023). While healthcare providers remain trusted sources of information, the constant barrage of contradictory statements and sensational headlines often drowns out expert advice, leading individuals to form opinions based on incomplete or inaccurate data.

The anxiety stemming from safety concerns inevitably affects workplace dynamics and morale. Employees worried about potential health impacts might experience stress and dissatisfaction, potentially affecting productivity and workplace harmony. Additionally, divisions may arise among staff who hold differing views on vaccination, causing friction and undermining team cohesion. Addressing these anxieties requires balancing educational efforts to dispel myths while respecting individual concerns. Open communication and empathetic engagement from employers could foster trust and address fears more effectively.

Legal cases highlight the complexities of accommodating both individual safety concerns and public health imperatives. Lawsuits filed by employees contesting mandatory vaccinations often underscore the need for clear criteria in addressing exemptions, supporting a transparent dialogue between employers and employees. Meanwhile, for some employees, understanding the extensive monitoring and stringent safety protocols established by regulatory authorities might mitigate concerns. Continuous updates on vaccine safety profiles and robust data-driven advocacy can play pivotal roles in changing perceptions over time.

Violation of Employment Contracts

Employment contracts present a substantial legal framework for challenging mandatory vaccination policies, offering employees an avenue to argue that such mandates infringe upon agreed-upon terms of employment. When examining contractual violations alleged by employees against compulsory vaccination, several key elements emerge as pivotal points in these disputes.

Firstly, the crux of employee arguments often revolves around specific contractual terms that they claim are breached by mandatory vaccinations. These terms might include clauses related to personal health choices and bodily autonomy as part of employment conditions. Employees may assert that these compulsory measures represent a unilateral modification of their contract, which originally did not stipulate mandatory medical procedures as a condition of employment. This perspective suggests that employers have reneged on the initial terms of employment agreements that respected the employees' right to control their own health decisions. In this context, it's vital for a clear understanding of whether the original contracts contained any language explicitly or implicitly guaranteeing the right to refuse medical interventions like vaccinations.

Illustrating instances where employment agreements have guaranteed personal health choices provides practical insights into how contracts can serve as defenses. Such instances often appear in industries with strong union representation, where collective bargaining agreements explicitly address health and safety protocols. For example, some contracts specify that decisions regarding medical procedures fall within the scope of individual discretion unless there is a clear, demonstrable threat to workplace safety. Cases abound where unions demand negotiations over changes to health-related policies, viewing mandatory vaccination as a term that alters working conditions significantly enough to warrant consent from employees.

The legal landscape around contract breaches related to health mandates is nuanced and informed by precedents set in court rulings. Courts evaluate these cases by considering both the letter of the contract and broader public health considerations. Noteworthy precedents include decisions where courts sided with employers, recognizing mandatory vaccination as legitimate under specific circumstances, especially when justified by the need to protect vulnerable populations. However, in cases where contractual language was sufficiently vague or supportive of employee autonomy, courts have occasionally ruled in favor of employees, affirming their rights to refuse vaccination without fearing job loss.

Assessing the effectiveness of contract-based arguments against workplace vaccination requirements reveals mixed outcomes. Success largely depends on the strength and clarity of the contractual language concerning health interventions. Contracts that include explicit provisions on employee choice regarding health matters tend to provide stronger grounds for legal challenges. On the contrary, general contracts without clear references to health autonomy often leave employees with weaker claims. Furthermore, the overarching public interest in maintaining workplace safety during a pandemic may diminish the potency of these arguments in court. Employers are expected to demonstrate that their vaccination mandates are a reasonable exercise of their duty to ensure a safe work environment, which often tips the scales in their favor.

For employees seeking to challenge vaccine mandates through contractual avenues, it is crucial to understand the complexities involved. They must first ascertain the presence of contractual terms supporting their stance. Legal experts often advise reviewing contracts thoroughly, looking for clauses that could be interpreted as recognizing personal health choices. In the absence of explicit language, employees might argue implicit understandings of autonomy based on past practices or verbal assurances, though these arguments typically face higher hurdles in court.

Discrimination under ADA

Exploring claims of discrimination under the Americans with Disabilities Act (ADA) provides a critical lens through which to examine the complexities of vaccine mandates in the workplace. The ADA, enacted in 1990, is designed to protect individuals with disabilities from discrimination in various facets of life, including employment. Its relevance has grown amidst the mandatory vaccination policies that have been implemented by employers in response to the COVID-19 pandemic.

To understand how the ADA interacts with vaccine mandates, it is essential to define what constitutes a disability under this law. According to the ADA, a disability is a physical or mental impairment that substantially limits one or more major life activities. This broad definition encompasses a wide variety of conditions, from chronic illnesses like diabetes and cancer to mental health disorders such as depression and anxiety. In the context of vaccination mandates, individuals who cannot be vaccinated due to medical conditions may qualify for protection under the ADA.

Legal arguments presented by employees claim that mandatory vaccination policies are discriminatory against those with specific medical conditions. For instance, an employee with a documented allergy to vaccine ingredients might argue that a blanket vaccination requirement fails to accommodate their disability. Under the ADA, employers must provide reasonable accommodations unless doing so would impose an undue hardship on the business. This legal framework sets the stage for lawsuits where employees assert that their rights have been violated when employers do not offer alternative measures, such as remote working options or regular testing, in lieu of vaccination.

An analysis of employer responsibilities under the ADA reveals the challenges businesses face in accommodating unvaccinated employees due to disabilities. Employers must engage in an interactive process with the employee to determine a suitable accommodation. This might include modifying work duties, allowing telecommuting, or implementing stringent safety protocols. However, the employer's duty to accommodate is balanced against the "direct threat" standard, articulated in EEOC guidance that determines if an unvaccinated employee could pose a significant risk to the health and safety of others in the workplace (EEOC, 2020).

The legal landscape becomes clearer when examining landmark cases where ADA claims have played a pivotal role in litigation over vaccine mandates. In these cases, the courts have deliberated on whether employers made adequate efforts to accommodate employees while also considering public health directives. One notable case involved healthcare employees who were unable to receive the flu vaccine due to medical reasons. Here, the court ruled that the employer had not sufficiently considered alternatives that would have allowed these employees to continue working safely without being vaccinated.

These cases highlight the importance of ensuring that employer policies align with ADA protections. They also underscore the necessity for employers to keep abreast of evolving public health guidelines, as the criteria for assessing a "direct threat" can shift based on the current understanding of diseases like COVID-19 and its variants.

The nuances of these legal battles illustrate the delicate balance between protecting public health and upholding individual rights. Employees seeking to challenge mandatory vaccination policies often face the burden of proving that they have a qualifying disability under the ADA and that their employer failed to provide reasonable accommodations. These cases frequently require substantial documentation and clear communication between the employee and employer. Moreover, the outcomes are influenced by current medical knowledge, which necessitates that parties involved stay informed about updates from authorities like the CDC and FDA.

Given the complexity and potential implications of ADA-based discrimination claims, it's vital for both employees and employers to seek knowledgeable legal counsel. Understanding the intricacies of the ADA, coupled with a commitment to fostering a collaborative environment for discussing accommodations, can mitigate conflicts and lead to more equitable solutions.

Unsafe Medical Intervention Claims

In exploring the implications of employers enforcing potentially unsafe medical interventions, we first need to define what constitutes an "unsafe medical intervention." Within workplace health policies, this phrase commonly refers to any medical procedure or treatment that carries a significant risk of adverse effects which employees may be mandated to undertake as a condition of their employment. The concept of 'safety' in medical interventions is heavily scrutinized and debated, especially when it comes to employer-mandated actions like vaccinations, which may not have uniformly recognized safety across diverse populations.

To navigate the landscape where these interventions are contested, employees have several legal avenues. One primary method involves challenging the intervention based on negligence or lack of due diligence by the employer in assessing risks. This can manifest as lawsuits where employees claim that their employer failed to provide adequate information about potential side effects or neglected to consider individual medical histories, thus rendering the intervention unsafe for certain individuals. Legal contingencies often pivot on demonstrating that the employer either knew, or should have known, about alternative methods to achieve workplace safety without imposing potentially harmful medical requirements.

Statistics and data on adverse reactions play a crucial role in substantiating these legal claims. For instance, the U.S. Occupational Safety and Health Administration's (OSHA) guidance demands that adverse reactions to vaccines must be recorded if the vaccination is required by the employer. This measure aims to hold employers accountable for any health outcomes resulting from mandatory vaccinations (OSHA Imposes New Guidance for Employer-Required COVID-19 Vaccines, n.d.). Recording such cases helps establish a pattern or prevalence of adverse reactions, providing empirical evidence that can influence court rulings. These records can show whether significant numbers of adverse reactions occur, offering a basis for questioning the safety of the mandated intervention.

Herein lies a critical tension between employer liability concerns and public health goals. Employers face potential liabilities if they enforce medical interventions that lead to negative health outcomes among employees. On one hand, they must ensure a safe work environment, aligning with public health imperatives to limit disease spread through vaccination mandates. On the other hand, they risk legal repercussions if those interventions harm employees or if the interventions are implemented without proper accommodations for individual health conditions.

Moreover, while some employers view mandatory vaccinations as vital for protecting workers and clients, others see it as a potential legal minefield. The construction industry, for example, has seen significant pushback against OSHA's guidance, with many contractors opting to recommend rather than require vaccinations due to fears of heightened legal exposure from adverse vaccine reactions (OSHA Imposes New Guidance for Employer-Required COVID-19 Vaccines, n.d.). Such decisions highlight the complex balance employers must maintain—protecting public health while mitigating liability risks.

Comparatively, public health goals emphasize widespread immunity to prevent disease outbreaks, sometimes in direct conflict with individual rights and safety concerns. The legal frameworks in place aim to protect both sides but often leave room for dispute interpretation, especially concerning what is deemed reasonable and necessary for ensuring collective safety.

Considering the intricacies involved, guidelines are essential for navigating these disputes. Employers must adhere to established health and safety protocols, ensuring they conduct thorough risk assessments and make informed decisions based on current medical data. Clear communication with employees about the benefits and potential risks associated with medical interventions is key. Employers should also accommodate individual health needs where possible and consult legal experts to align policies with both federal and state regulations to mitigate risks ('Employers knowingly enforcing an unsafe medical intervention').

Final Insights

In this chapter, we've journeyed through the legal maze employees navigate when opposing mandatory vaccinations. Beyond religious grounds, personal safety concerns, medical autonomy, and misinformation play significant roles in fueling hesitancy. Employees are not just voices in the dark; they are pivotal players facing real dilemmas as workplaces enforce vaccination policies. These issues come with no easy answers, highlighting a delicate balance between maintaining a safe work environment and respecting individual choices. Legal battles reveal not just disagreements but deep-seated fears surrounding health decisions that can impact job security and personal well-being.

By exploring various legal claims—from contractual breaches to ADA discrimination and unsafe medical interventions—we've shed light on the complexities confronting those challenging vaccine mandates. The narrative isn't merely about vaccines but about broader themes of autonomy, trust, and rights within employment settings. For healthcare workers, first responders, and diverse political voices, it's a shared struggle for clarity in chaotic times. As we try to understand both sides, it's clear that ongoing dialogue and thoughtful consideration of legal precedents are essential in navigating these workplace challenges.

Reference List

(2023). Bloomberglaw.com. https://www.bloomberglaw.com/external/document/X5QSND48000000/employment-checklist-considerations-for-employer-mandated-covid-

Chirico, F., & Teixeira da Silva, J. A. (2023, April 4). Evidence-based policies in public health to address COVID-19 vaccine hesitancy. Future Virology. https://doi.org/10.2217/fvl-2022-0028

EEOC. (2020, December 16). What You Should Know About COVID-19 and the ADA, the Rehabilitation Act, and Other EEO Laws | U.S. Equal Employment Opportunity Commission. Www.eeoc.gov. https://www.eeoc.gov/wysk/what-you-should-know-about-covid-19-and-ada-rehabilitation-act-and-other-eeo-laws

Flood, C. M., Thomas, B., & Wilson, K. (2021, January 19). Mandatory vaccination for health care workers: an analysis of law and policy. Canadian Medical Association Journal. https://doi.org/10.1503/cmaj.202755

Goje, O., & Kapoor, A. (2024, September 1). Meeting the challenge of vaccine hesitancy. Cleveland Clinic Journal of Medicine; Cleveland Clinic. https://doi.org/10.3949/ccjm.91.s1.08

OSHA Imposes New Guidance For Employer-Required COVID-19 Vaccines. (n.d.). Www.enr.com. https://www.enr.com/articles/51691-osha-imposes-new-guidance-for-employer-required-covid-19-vaccines

Rothstein, M. A., Parmet, W. E., & Reiss, D. R. (2021, February 4). Employer-Mandated Vaccination for COVID-19. American Journal of Public Health. https://doi.org/10.2105/ajph.2020.306166

Regulations.gov. (2025). Regulations.gov. https://www.regulations.gov/document/OSHA-2021-0008-0001

Part IV: The Step-by-Step Guide to Suing Your Employer

Chapter 7 How to File a Wrongful Termination Lawsuit for Vaccine Refusal

Filing a wrongful termination lawsuit because of vaccine refusal might sound daunting, but with the right approach, it's certainly achievable. If you've lost your job or faced significant pressure at work due to your stance on COVID-19 vaccinations, this chapter is designed to be your guide through the sometimes complicated terrain of legal actions and rights. For many, especially those in high-stakes professions like healthcare workers, first responders, and military personnel, understanding how to move forward after dismissal can be critical not only for personal justice but also as a stand against what some might view as overreaching policies.

In this chapter, readers will uncover the practical steps needed to gather evidence for their case, from documenting communications to identifying patterns within their workplace that might suggest unfair treatment. Insight into understanding the types of lawsuits available and choosing the right one for your situation is key. Furthermore, we'll discuss strategies for seeking qualified legal representation and engaging with class-action lawsuits, including advice on finding lawyers who specialize in vaccine-related employment cases. By the end, you should feel equipped with a comprehensive strategy and the confidence to take informed steps, should you decide to pursue legal action, supported by robust documentation and a thorough grasp of your rights and options.

Gathering Essential Evidence

When building a case for wrongful termination due to vaccine refusal, gathering the right documentation is crucial. Start by collecting all relevant emails, termination letters, and HR communications. These documents are vital as they provide evidence of your employment status and the specific circumstances surrounding your termination. Emails often contain essential details and timelines that outline the communication between you and your employer, clarifying any misunderstandings or disputes. A termination letter, on the other hand, formally documents the reasons provided by the employer for ending your employment and serves as an official record should there be discrepancies later on (18 Employee Termination Letter Samples Based on Reasons, 2023).

Furthermore, it's essential to identify any coworkers who also refused the vaccine and document their outcomes. This step is key in establishing patterns or precedents that may support your claim of unfair treatment. For example, if multiple employees were in similar positions but faced different consequences, it could indicate inconsistency in how company policies were applied. Documenting these cases—whether through firsthand accounts, testimonies, or patterns observed within the organization—can strengthen your argument that your termination was not isolated but perhaps part of a broader issue.

Obtaining copies of your employment contract and any pertinent company policies is another critical step. Your employment contract outlines the terms of your engagement, responsibilities, and conditions under which termination might occur. Reviewing this document can reveal whether your termination violated any agreed-upon terms or if the company failed to adhere to its stated policies regarding vaccine mandates or accommodations. Company policies, especially those recently updated to accommodate pandemic-related measures, will show whether they were followed correctly or selectively enforced at the time of your termination (Team, 2024).

In addition to written documentation, recording any verbal exchanges related to the decision to terminate your employment is beneficial. These records provide indispensable context that can complement the formal documents you've gathered. Verbal exchanges, when documented accurately, can shed light on nuances not captured in writing, such as tone, intent, and additional information conveyed during conversations. It might be helpful to keep a journal of these interactions, noting dates, participants, and the essence of what was discussed. Voice memos or detailed notes taken immediately after conversations can serve as valuable evidence in painting a fuller picture of the circumstances leading to your dismissal.

Each piece of documentation plays a distinct role in strengthening your case. By meticulously compiling all these documents, you create a comprehensive narrative that supports your claim. Providing clear, detailed evidence not only substantiates your allegations but also challenges the credibility of any counter-narrative presented by your employer. The goal is to ensure that your case is robust, transparent, and persuasive by relying on factual evidence that underscores the legitimacy of your grievance against wrongful termination.

Identifying the Right Type of Lawsuit

When navigating the complexities of a wrongful termination lawsuit due to vaccine refusal, understanding and choosing an appropriate legal path is essential. Employees who face termination for refusing COVID-19 vaccination must first determine whether their dismissal qualifies as wrongful based on discrimination related to personal health choices.

To begin, assess if your situation meets the criteria for a wrongful termination claim under discrimination laws. Federal regulations, such as Title VII of the Civil Rights Act of 1964, prohibit employment discrimination based on factors like race, sex, religion, and national origin (Sullivan, 2020). Additionally, laws protect against discrimination due to age and disability. If you feel that your termination was influenced by biases linked to your personal health decisions or any protected category, it may be prudent to file a complaint with the Equal Employment Opportunity Commission (EEOC).

Next, evaluate whether your employer has violated specific labor laws that safeguard employee rights in certain conditions. Labor laws can vary significantly from state to state, but many of these statutes are designed to shield workers from unjust treatment and preserve fair workplace practices. For instance, employees might have protections relating to working conditions and safety, which could apply if vaccine mandates infringe upon negotiated agreements or customary employment standards. Consulting with a knowledgeable employment attorney can provide clarity about whether labor law violations occurred in your case (Sullivan, 2020).

Additionally, consider whether there have been instances of retaliation leading up to your termination. Retaliation can occur if you reported or opposed unlawful activities and subsequently faced adverse job actions, such as demotion or harassment before being fired. Termination following such protected activities may indicate retaliatory motives, offering grounds for a separate lawsuit. Under the Whistleblower Protections, employees who disclose unethical workplace issues or refuse illegal demands should not suffer negative employment consequences (Firing / Wrongful Termination, 2018).

Breaches of implied contracts or established company norms can also strengthen your legal standing. Although most employment is considered at-will, meaning employers can generally terminate employees without cause, exceptions exist if implied agreements are breached. For example, if a handbook specifies a progressive discipline policy, such as issuing three warnings before termination, and this process was not followed, it could represent a breach of implied contract. Employees should meticulously review any employment contracts, handbooks, or relevant company policies to identify potential breaches that might fortify their case. When an employee's dismissal contradicts previous assurances or standard procedures, it can serve as evidence in a wrongful termination claim.

Recognizing these elements paves the way for making informed decisions regarding the legal path that fits your individual circumstances. Your steps will involve gathering substantial evidence to support claims of discrimination, retaliation, or contract breaches. Documenting everything meticulously—from emails and written communications with HR to any verbal exchanges surrounding your termination—becomes crucial for building a strong case (Sullivan, 2020). Evidence showing differential treatment or inconsistencies between stated policies and your experience will be vital for contesting your dismissal effectively.

While exploring your options, weigh the importance of obtaining professional legal guidance. An experienced wrongful termination lawyer can help untangle the complex web of employment rights and manage the intricacies of litigation (Sullivan, 2020). They play a pivotal role in recognizing viable claims, collecting admissible evidence, and presenting a coherent narrative during proceedings.

Seeking Qualified Legal Representation

When faced with wrongful termination due to vaccine refusal, it is crucial to secure competent legal assistance. Finding the right lawyer can make a significant difference in the outcome of your case. Start by researching employment lawyers who specialize in vaccine mandates and related terminations. These professionals possess specific expertise in navigating the intricacies of such cases and can offer invaluable guidance.

Consider using online legal directories or reaching out to local bar associations for recommendations. Focus on locating attorneys with a proven track record in handling similar disputes, as this experience will inform their strategic approach to your case. Engaging an expert will not only increase your chances of success but also provide peace of mind throughout the process.

Joining class-action lawsuits is another avenue worth exploring. By collaborating with others facing similar challenges, you can leverage collective strength and share resources. Class actions consolidate multiple individual claims into one lawsuit, leading to more efficient proceedings. Additionally, participating in a class-action suit might reduce legal expenses, offering a cost-effective solution for seeking justice.

Investigate ongoing class-action lawsuits related to vaccine mandate terminations either through news articles or legal websites specializing in employment law. Understanding the specifics of these cases will help you determine whether joining is a viable option. However, be sure to consult with your attorney to assess if a class action aligns with your best interests and personal circumstances.

Filing a complaint with the Equal Employment Opportunity Commission (EEOC) is another crucial step in addressing potential workplace rights infringements. The EEOC enforces laws prohibiting employment discrimination based on various factors, including religion and disability, which may be applicable in vaccine-related termination cases. Familiarize yourself with the process of filing a complaint to ensure that your rights are protected.

Start by visiting the EEOC website or contacting your nearest office for detailed information on how to file a charge of discrimination (EEOC, 2020).

You must adhere to specific timelines and procedures to maintain your claim's viability. Consider consulting with your attorney during this phase to navigate any complexities that may arise and to ensure your complaint accurately reflects your situation.

Assessing the track record and reputation of potential lawyers is essential in securing quality representation. A lawyer's history of successful outcomes in similar cases can demonstrate their capability and dedication to their clients' causes. When evaluating candidates, consider their experience, client reviews, and professional credentials.

Requesting references from former clients or reading testimonials can provide insight into a lawyer's performance and communication skills. Remember, effective representation goes beyond legal acumen; it encompasses the ability to empathize with your situation and advocate passionately on your behalf.

Strategizing the Legal Process

When embarking on the journey of filing a wrongful termination lawsuit for vaccine refusal, it's crucial to create a detailed plan that guides you through each stage of the legal proceedings. This begins with establishing realistic expectations regarding both the timeline and potential outcomes of your case. Historically, wrongful termination lawsuits can be lengthy processes; some may span months or even years before reaching a resolution. Drawing parallels from past cases, one should understand that though victories are possible, they often require patience and resilience. For example, in cases involving claims of discrimination based on religious beliefs or medical exemptions, challenges arise due to varying interpretations of legal protections under laws like Title VII or the Americans with Disabilities Act (Hunton, 2023). Therefore, setting sensible goals regarding timelines and potential verdicts will help maintain clarity throughout the process.

Preparation is a cornerstone of success in any legal dispute. To build a solid foundation for mediation sessions or courtroom hearings, compiling comprehensive evidence is essential. Begin by gathering documentation such as correspondence and records relating to your employment and termination circumstances. Additionally, crafting a compelling narrative that clearly outlines how the termination was wrongful is vital. This story should integrate all aspects of the event—why you refused the vaccine, how the refusal led to termination, and why this action was discriminatory or unjust according to existing laws. By doing so, you paint a vivid picture that aids those involved in understanding your position. Evidence in similar cases, such as those involving other mandates or employment rights disputes, can also bolster your argument if presented effectively (EEOC, 2020).

Staying informed about current labor laws and updates around vaccine mandates is another critical component of navigating these proceedings. Laws and legal opinions are dynamic, especially in areas affected by recent events like COVID-19. Regulatory bodies frequently update guidelines that might influence your case's strength or strategic direction. Regularly reviewing announcements from agencies such as the Equal Employment Opportunity Commission (EEOC) or following landmark court decisions helps you adapt your approach proactively. Keeping abreast of changes ensures that your claims remain relevant and legally sound. It aligns your strategies with the most recent legal precedents, fortifying your case against potential counterarguments from your former employer.

Regular coordination with your legal team cannot be overstated. Effective communication guarantees that all tactical elements align seamlessly with emerging developments in your case. It's advisable to schedule frequent meetings or check-ins to discuss progress, review new information, and tweak tactics where necessary. This collaboration helps you meet procedural requirements promptly, preventing any missed deadlines that could jeopardize your lawsuit. More importantly, it offers space to address concerns and explore alternative approaches as new circumstances unfold. In navigating complex legal landscapes, having a team well-versed in employment law on your side, one that remains engaged and supportive, is invaluable.

Additionally, consider leveraging the expertise of professionals who have historically handled cases related to vaccine mandates. Lawyers specializing in employment law with exposure to termination cases based on personal health choices have the nuanced understanding required to navigate these waters (Hunton, 2023). Their familiarity with common judicial interpretations and likely defense arguments provides an edge that general practitioners might lack.

Moreover, the insight from such specialists can illuminate the subtleties of labor regulations or exception clauses pertinent to your situation.

In certain scenarios, joining forces with others through class-action lawsuits can be advantageous. Class actions allow individuals facing similar issues to pool resources, share burdens, and present consolidated claims against employers. This collective approach not only strengthens bargaining power but also spreads legal costs over a larger group, potentially reducing financial strain for each participant. If suitable, exploring this option with guidance from your lawyer may broaden avenues for recourse while maximizing your chances of a favorable outcome.

Final Analysis

Understanding the many steps in filing a wrongful termination lawsuit due to vaccine refusal is undoubtedly complex but crucial. This chapter guided you through building a strong foundation by collecting essential evidence and choosing the right legal path. The journey begins with gathering documents, such as emails and termination letters, which form the backbone of your claim. Identifying coworkers who faced similar challenges strengthens your case by highlighting patterns of unfair treatment. Reviewing employment contracts and company policies ensures that your rights are safeguarded. With all this information in hand, assessing whether discrimination laws protect you sets the stage for your legal battle. Labor laws vary, so understanding your local protections is vital, and consulting with an experienced attorney can clarify the nuances.

The emotional toll of wrongful termination and the intricacies of legal proceedings underline the importance of involving skilled legal professionals. This chapter also emphasized seeking capable representation, researching qualified lawyers, and considering collective actions like class-action lawsuits. Filing complaints with bodies like the EEOC offers avenues to address potential rights infringements, and maintaining a collaborative relationship with your legal team propels your case forward. Engaging strategically, staying informed about current regulations, and coordinating regularly with experts help navigate this challenging landscape. While each step requires diligence, it's achievable with focused efforts and a proactive approach. Empowered with knowledge and armed with a detailed strategy, tackling wrongful termination is within your grasp.

Reference List

18 Employee Termination Letter Samples Based on Reasons. (2023). Keka HR. https://www.keka.com/termination-email-template

EEOC. (2020, December 16). What You Should Know About COVID-19 and the ADA, the Rehabilitation Act, and Other EEO Laws | U.S. Equal Employment Opportunity Commission. Www.eeoc.gov. https://www.eeoc.gov/wysk/what-you-should-know-about-covid-19-and-ada-rehabilitation-act-and-other-eeo-laws

Firing / Wrongful Termination. (2018, September 26). Justia. https://www.justia.com/employment/hiring-employment-contracts/firing-wrongful-termination/

Hunton. (2023, December 12). COVID Vaccine Class Action Reminds Employers to Individually Consider Accommodations. @HuntonAK. https://www.hunton.com/hunton-employment-labor-perspectives/covid-vaccine-class-action-reminds-employers-to-individually-consider-accommodations

Sullivan, K. (2020, August 18). MORE GOOD NEWS FOR LGBTQ COMMUNITY. Barrett & Farahany; Barrett and Farahany. https://www.justiceatwork.com/what-are-the-types-of-wrongful-termination/

Team, T. R. (2024, November 6). 5 Termination Letter to Employee Templates & Tips [2024] | Rippling. Rippling. https://www.rippling.com/blog/termination-letter

Chapter 8 What to Expect After Filing Your Lawsuit

Filing a lawsuit can feel like entering uncharted waters, filled with uncertainty about what's to come. Many individuals find themselves overwhelmed by the legal process and concerned about potential repercussions from their employers. This chapter explores the steps involved after taking legal action and aims to demystify what follows, helping would-be plaintiffs understand what they might encounter on this journey. From initial filings to settlement discussions or trials, each stage comes with its own set of expectations and possible outcomes. The decision to file a lawsuit is often driven by a need for justice or resolution, but it also opens the door to various challenges that require careful navigation.

This chapter delves into the intricacies of filing a lawsuit, providing readers with insights into different phases they will face. Readers will learn about the potential for employer retaliation and how to protect themselves from negative consequences such as blacklisting or damaging references. Discussing the settlement process outlines what compensation one might expect if victorious, while comparing the pros and cons of going to trial versus settling gives critical context for making informed decisions. Additionally, guidance on rebuilding life post-litigation supports efforts to restore one's career and reputation. By breaking down these aspects, this chapter equips those affected by wrongful termination due to vaccine mandates, and others seeking accountability, with knowledge and confidence to pursue their legal rights.

Employer Retaliation: How to Protect Yourself Against Blacklisting and Negative References

Protecting Yourself from Employer Retaliation After Filing a Lawsuit

Filing a lawsuit against an employer can be a daunting step, often necessary to address workplace injustices. However, it unfortunately may expose employees to retaliation. Understanding how to protect yourself is crucial, and here's how you can achieve that.

Firstly, identifying and documenting any instances of retaliation or negative references by the employer is vital. Retaliation can manifest in various ways, such as demotions, pay cuts, or subtle actions like social isolation at work. Documenting these acts with dates, times, and descriptions will create a comprehensive record should the need arise to present evidence. For example, if your supervisor suddenly excludes you from important meetings after learning about your legal action, make detailed notes including who was present and what was discussed. This meticulously gathered information forms the backbone of any complaint you might file under laws protecting against retaliation (What Is Retaliation? | Whistleblower Protection Program, n.d.).

Furthermore, it's imperative to learn your legal rights and remedies under specific protections like the Whistleblower Protection Act or other anti-retaliation clauses inherent in employment law. These laws are designed to shield employees from punitive actions when they report violations of law. The U.S. Department of Labor (DOL) oversees numerous offices ensuring these protections, including the Occupational Safety and Health Administration (OSHA) and the Office of Federal Contract Compliance Programs (OFCCP). These bodies provide guidelines on recognizing and addressing retaliation, thus equipping employees with the knowledge needed to seek appropriate recourse (U.S. Department of Labor, 2023).

To further safeguard your position, you should consider implementing preventative measures. This includes seeking guidance from employment lawyers who specialize in labor disputes. A seasoned attorney can provide tailored advice, help you understand your rights comprehensively, and assist in strategizing the best course of action. They can also ensure that any communication with your employer or third parties is legally sound and does not inadvertently weaken your case.

Another proactive approach is developing strategies for career resilience. This involves networking extensively within your industry both before and during any legal proceedings. Engaging actively with professional associations and forums can enhance your visibility and connect you with potential new employers. Furthermore, securing supportive references from previous employers or colleagues can bolster your reputation. This strategy can prove invaluable, especially if your current employer attempts to blacklist you or provide negative references to prospective employers. Being a whistleblower should not cost you future opportunities, and having verifiable support from past employers can counteract any detrimental effects of your current situation.

It's essential to realize that while the threat of retaliation is real, tools and resources are available to support you. Many organizations and advocacy groups focus on employee rights and can offer additional guidance and support as you navigate this challenging terrain. They can connect you with legal experts, provide educational resources on handling workplace issues, and sometimes even offer mental health support or counseling services for dealing with the stress associated with legal battles.

The Settlement Process: What Compensation You Can Expect If You Win

In the aftermath of filing a lawsuit, understanding the settlement process and potential compensation outcomes is crucial for navigating the legal landscape effectively. This section delves into the nuances that can impact settlement amounts and explores potential components of a settlement agreement, offering insight into expectations after initiating legal action.

Several factors influence settlement amounts, with case strength being one of the foremost considerations. A strong case, characterized by compelling evidence and clear documentation, often results in higher settlement offers. Plaintiffs who can demonstrate undeniable harm or violation may leverage this advantage in negotiations. The damages claimed play a significant role as well; quantifiable losses such as lost wages, medical expenses, and emotional distress are critical in determining fair compensation. These tangible and intangible losses must be meticulously documented to justify the claimed amount during the negotiation phase. Furthermore, seasoned negotiation tactics by legal representatives can steer discussions favorably, impacting final settlement terms positively.

Settlements typically include various components, each serving distinct purposes. Monetary compensation is the most common settlement element, addressing direct financial losses incurred by the plaintiff. However, settlements can also encompass non-monetary benefits. Reinstatement of employment, apologies, or policy changes within organizations may be included to address grievances beyond financial constraints. In cases involving wrongful termination, for instance, reinstatement might be prioritized, ensuring continued income and professional stability for the affected employee.

Mediation plays a pivotal role in achieving agreeable settlements without resorting to trial. As a structured, facilitated negotiation process, mediation encourages open dialogue between parties in a neutral setting. By focusing on collaborative problem-solving, mediation helps parties reach mutual agreements that reflect their underlying interests, often leading to more satisfactory outcomes than adversarial courtroom battles. It offers an opportunity to explore creative solutions tailored to both parties' needs, fostering a sense of control over the resolution process, which is often absent in litigation.

The tax implications of settlement funds add another layer of complexity to the process, necessitating careful consideration. Settlements can have significant tax consequences depending on the nature of the compensation. For instance, awards intended to replace lost income are generally considered taxable, while certain personal injury damages may be excluded from taxation. Consulting with financial advisors or tax professionals is advisable to navigate these implications accurately, ensuring compliance with tax laws and optimizing the net benefit of the settlement received. The origin-of-the-claim test is instrumental in determining the appropriate tax treatment—whether payments should be regarded as ordinary income or capital gain. More flexibility exists in ensuring the proper tax characterization when litigation concludes with a settlement rather than a court judgment (Sorting the Tax Consequences of Settlements and Judgments, 2021).

The focus on settlements extends to pragmatic considerations around how they are structured. While lump-sum settlements provide immediate financial relief, caution is necessary to avoid financial mismanagement (Understanding Workers' Compensation Settlements, 2024). Structured settlements, offering periodic payments, mitigate this risk by ensuring steady income over time, albeit with reduced flexibility. In choosing between these options, plaintiffs must weigh their current financial needs against long-term security, ideally with guidance from financial advisors who can tailor strategies to individual circumstances.

Going to Trial vs. Settling: Pros and Cons of Fighting Your Case in Court

When deciding between going to trial or settling out of court, it's vital to weigh the potential for higher compensation against the costs involved. Trials often promise the possibility of receiving a larger financial award compared to settlements. The reason is simple: juries can be swayed by emotional appeals and might award damages that exceed what insurance companies are willing to offer during pre-trial negotiations. In personal injury cases, for instance, trial verdicts might include punitive damages designed to punish the defendant, which are not typically available in settlements (Firm, 2023).

However, the road to obtaining potentially higher compensation through a trial is fraught with challenges. First, the financial burden cannot be overlooked. Trials are inherently costly due to legal fees, expert witness testimonies, and other associated expenses. These costs can quickly accumulate, making the trial financially burdensome. Prolonged litigation also translates to more time spent dealing with the stress and emotional toll of the legal process, impacting both the plaintiff and their family. For individuals already facing financial hardships because of job terminations or medical bills, this added stress can be significant (Group, 2024).

In contrast, opting for a settlement offers more certainty and speed. Settlements are often resolved much faster than trials, allowing plaintiffs to receive their compensation sooner. This quick resolution is particularly appealing to those who need immediate financial relief. Furthermore, settlements come with fewer risks. By accepting an agreed-upon amount, plaintiffs eliminate the uncertainty of a trial outcome where there's always a chance the verdict could favor the defendant. This certainty provides a sense of closure that can be essential for emotional recovery.

Nevertheless, there is a trade-off when it comes to public exposure and setting precedents. Trials are public records; they allow plaintiffs to bring attention to their case, hold defendants publicly accountable, and sometimes set legal precedents that benefit future claimants. For example, high-profile cases can highlight unlawful corporate policies or discriminatory practices, driving change beyond the individual case. On the flip side, private settlement agreements keep cases out of the limelight, preserving confidentiality but leaving broader issues unaddressed and defendants unaccountable in the public eye (Firm, 2023).

Another consideration is how each option influences relationships with defendants or insurers. Trials can strain these relationships further due to their adversarial nature, while settlements may preserve them through negotiation and compromise. This can be crucial for parties who have ongoing interactions or need to maintain long-term professional relationships.

In assessing whether to go to trial or settle, one must consider the strength of their evidence and likelihood of success at trial. Strong evidence can bolster a case, increasing the chances of achieving a favorable jury verdict. Conversely, weak evidence might make a settlement more attractive, as it minimizes the risk of an adverse trial result.

Navigating Post-Lawsuit Life: Rebuilding Careers and Reputations

Restoring your career and professional reputation after a lawsuit can be a challenging journey, but with the right strategies, it's entirely possible to regain your footing. The first step involves implementing concrete career rebuilding strategies that focus on skill enhancement and proactive job searching. Skill enhancement can serve as a powerful way to stay competitive in today's job market. Consider taking courses or certifications that are relevant to your field and demonstrate your commitment to continuous learning. Online platforms offer numerous free and paid resources where you can learn new skills or deepen existing ones. By actively upgrading your expertise, you not only widen your employment opportunities but also reinforce your professional image as someone who values growth and adaptation.

Proactive job searching is equally vital. This means tailoring your resume and cover letters to each job application, highlighting not just your skills and experiences but also any new qualifications you've acquired during this rebuilding phase. Leverage job search engines and professional networks to explore potential job openings that align with your career goals. It's also crucial to practice interview skills. Prepare to discuss your lawsuit experience in a manner that emphasizes what you learned and how it has prepared you for future challenges. This approach can help shift any potential employer focus from the lawsuit itself to your resilience and readiness for new opportunities.

Meanwhile, engaging in rehabilitating relationships within your industry can significantly aid in restoring your professional standing. This might involve reconnecting with former colleagues or mentors, attending industry conferences, and participating in relevant professional networks. Engaging in these activities can help rebuild trust and connections that may have been strained due to the lawsuit. Networking can open doors to new opportunities and provide valuable insights into industry trends. Actively contribute to discussions or offer to assist in projects where your expertise could be beneficial. Demonstrating your willingness to collaborate and support others can go a long way in mending professional relationships.

Developing a narrative about your lawsuit experience is another important aspect of restoring your career and reputation. It's essential to craft a story that honestly addresses the events leading up to the lawsuit, while equally emphasizing personal growth, resilience, and the positive outcomes that followed. This narrative should be framed positively and professionally, allowing you to steer conversations with potential employers or industry peers toward your strengths and aspirations. Practicing how you communicate this narrative will help in interviews and networking situations, ensuring that you present yourself as a strong candidate ready to move forward.

Lastly, recognizing the mental health impacts of lawsuits is crucial. Legal processes can be emotionally taxing, often leading to stress and anxiety. Seeking counseling or joining support groups can provide much-needed emotional recovery and help manage these effects. Professional counseling offers a safe space to work through emotions and develop coping strategies, which can boost confidence when re-entering the workforce. Support groups allow you to connect with individuals facing similar situations, providing mutual understanding and encouragement.

Emphasizing self-care is an important part of recovering emotionally and mentally post-lawsuit, as highlighted by Sovold et al. (2021). Incorporate relaxation techniques, exercise, and mindfulness practices into your daily routine. These actions promote physical and mental well-being, fostering resilience as you navigate the challenges of career restoration. Maintaining a balanced lifestyle with proper nutrition, sleep, and recreational activities further supports emotional healing.

To summarize, while the aftermath of a lawsuit can seem daunting, it also presents an opportunity for personal and professional renewal. Through strategic skill enhancement, proactive job searching, relationship rehabilitation, crafting a positive narrative, and prioritizing mental health, you can effectively rebuild your career and reputation. Engaging with professional networks and continuously developing your skill set reflects a proactive approach that potential employers will recognize and appreciate. Remember, resilience and adaptability are key traits valued in any professional setting. By focusing on these areas, you're not just repairing past damage; you're building a stronger foundation for future success.

Bringing It All Together

Filing a lawsuit can be an overwhelming decision, especially when facing potential retaliation from employers. This chapter sheds light on the intricacies involved in such situations and highlights essential steps to safeguard your rights. It's crucial for individuals to document any retaliatory actions meticulously and understand their legal protections, like those offered by whistleblower acts. Seeking advice from specialized employment lawyers can provide invaluable guidance, while networking within your industry can help maintain career momentum despite ongoing legal actions. Remember, resources and support systems exist to assist you through these challenges, preventing unjust treatment from overshadowing your professional future.

Additionally, the chapter emphasized the importance of understanding the settlement process and its implications. Settlements often offer quicker, less risky resolutions compared to trials, but each path has its pros and cons that must be carefully weighed. For those considering the aftermath of litigation, focusing on rebuilding skills and professional connections is key. Emphasizing growth and resilience not only aids in personal recovery but enhances career prospects too. As challenging as these circumstances may be, they also present opportunities for renewal and advocacy against unjust practices, helping carve a more equitable path forward for yourself and others in similar situations.

Reference List

7 Second Resume. (2024). Navigating Job Loss: How to Approach Being Let Go... 7 Second Resume. https://7secondresume.com/f/navigating-job-loss-how-to-approach-being-let-go

Firm, S. L. (2023, December 26). Trial vs. Settlement: Pros and Cons in Michigan Personal Injury Cases. Sigal Law Firm. https://www.sigallaw.com/blog/trial-vs-settlement-pros-and-cons-in-michigan-personal-injury-cases/

Group, L. L. (2024, August 31). Personal Injury Settlements vs. Court Trials: Pros and Cons. Lanier Law Group, P.A. https://www.lanierlawgroup.com/blog/2024/august/personal-injury-settlements-vs-court-trials-pros/

Sorting the tax consequences of settlements and judgments. (2021, July 1). The Tax Adviser. https://www.thetaxadviser.com/issues/2021/jul/tax-consequences-settlements-judgments.html

Sovold, L. E., Naslund, J. A., Kousoulis, A. A., Saxena, S., Qoronfleh, M. W., Grobler, C., & Münter, L. (2021, May 7). Prioritizing the Mental Health and well-being of Healthcare workers: an Urgent Global Public Health Priority. Frontiers in Public Health. https://www.frontiersin.org/journals/public-health/articles/10.3389/fpubh.2021.679397/full

U.S. Department of Labor. (2023). Whistleblower Protections | U.S. Department of Labor. Www.dol.gov. https://www.dol.gov/general/topics/whistleblower

Understanding Workers' Compensation Settlements. (2024, September 17). Cole Fisher Cole O'Keefe + Mahoney. Cole Fisher Cole O'Keefe + Mahoney. https://colefisher.com/blog/understanding-workers-compensation-settlements

What Is Retaliation? | Whistleblower Protection Program. (n.d.). Www.whistleblowers.gov. https://www.whistleblowers.gov/know_your_rights

Part V: Moving Forward—Holding Employers Accountable

Chapter 9 Reinstating Your Job or Getting Compensation

Securing job reinstatement or compensation is a journey often fraught with complexity and challenge. When a court ruling favors an employee who has been wrongfully terminated, the process of returning to work or receiving financial reparation begins in earnest. Whether you're seeking to reclaim your former position or negotiating for what you believe you're owed, understanding the nuances of this process is critical. The paths to reinstatement or compensation vary greatly, involving legal frameworks, evidence gathering, and sometimes even negotiation with parties who might be resistant to a straightforward resolution.

In this chapter, we'll guide you through the intricate steps involved in achieving job reinstatement following a favorable court decision. We'll discuss the importance of aligning your actions with the relevant labor laws and provide insight into the documentation and evidence crucial for supporting your case. From gathering employment contracts and performance reviews to understanding how employers might resist reinstatement, you'll gain practical tips on navigating these hurdles. We will also delve into calculating lost wages as part of receiving compensation, ensuring you account for all potential earnings you missed due to wrongful termination. By the end, you'll have a clearer roadmap for addressing these issues, whether your goal is to return to work or secure the compensation to which you are entitled.

Process of Job Reinstatement

Obtaining job reinstatement after a favorable court ruling involves navigating a complex process filled with legal and procedural elements. This journey requires understanding the legal framework that governs job reinstatement under labor laws. The foundation of the reinstatement scenario lies in these laws, which vary by jurisdiction but generally aim to provide redress for wrongful terminations. Labor laws are designed to protect employees from unjust dismissals and outline circumstances under which reinstatement is appropriate.

Reinstatement is typically awarded when a court finds that an employee was terminated without just cause or in violation of specific legal protections, such as those against discrimination or retaliation. The criteria for reinstatement often depend on proving that the termination breached employment rights or violated contract terms. It's important to consult the relevant labor laws in your jurisdiction to understand the exact parameters that apply to your case. It is crucial to align any claims and actions with these legal standards to enhance the chances of successful reinstatement.

Once you grasp the legal framework, the next step is gathering documentation and evidence essential for the reinstatement process. Necessary documents may include the original employment contract, correspondence regarding the termination, performance reviews, and any relevant communications that support your claim. Evidence plays a pivotal role in demonstrating that your termination was unjust and warrants reinstatement. Gathering comprehensive documentation is a critical step, given that courts rely heavily on concrete evidence to make decisions.

Compile all communication records, whether emails, letters, or memos, between you and your employer, especially those leading up to and following your termination. Additionally, witness statements from colleagues or other individuals with firsthand knowledge of your situation can supplement documentary evidence. These testimonials can offer insights into workplace dynamics and bolster your case.

Despite a favorable court ruling, potential challenges and opposition from employers during the reinstatement process should be anticipated. It's common for employers to resist reinstatement due to factors such as workplace dynamics or managerial decisions that have occurred since the termination. Employers might argue that reinstating an employee would disrupt business operations or affect morale.

To overcome these challenges, it's crucial to leverage legal representation or dispute resolution mechanisms like mediation. Legal counsel can negotiate on your behalf, ensuring that your reinstatement complies with both the court's order and operational needs. Mediation offers an alternative path where both parties can reach a mutually agreeable solution, sometimes involving reinstatement with modifications or alternate compensation.

Understanding the timeline and procedural nuances involved in executing a reinstatement order is another critical aspect. The execution timeline begins once a court issues the reinstatement order, and can vary significantly depending on the complexity of the case and employer compliance. Generally, the court will specify time frames for compliance, and employers are legally obligated to adhere to these deadlines.

Procedural steps often include formal notification to the employer about the court's decision and outlining how the reinstatement should occur. It's important to maintain open lines of communication to ensure clarity and prevent misunderstandings. Sometimes, transition plans need to be developed, especially if significant time has passed since the employee's termination. Transitioning back into the workplace smoothly can involve discussions about role adjustments, training, or updates on company policies and systems that may have changed in your absence.

Given the multifaceted nature of obtaining job reinstatement post-court ruling, having clear guidelines is beneficial. Guidelines can offer structured steps to follow, reducing uncertainty and enhancing efficiency. They provide a roadmap that aligns with legal requirements, helping employees navigate the process systematically.

Calculating Lost Wages

Lost wages represent a crucial component in the context of financial damages when seeking compensation for wrongful termination. They are distinct from other forms of compensation such as benefits, which might include health insurance, retirement contributions, or additional perks tied to employment. The primary focus here is on the tangible income lost due to involuntary job loss.

To accurately calculate lost wages, we must first consider regular wages. This involves computing the amount you would have earned had you remained employed during the period between your dismissal and the court ruling. The formula typically reflects your gross salary over this period, considering any regularly scheduled raises that were missed.

Overtime wages also play an essential role. If your previous employment involved consistent overtime, these extra hours — often at an increased pay rate — should be included in the calculations. Documentation showing historical overtime patterns can support these claims, providing a robust case for their inclusion.

In addition to regular and overtime wages, missed bonuses need consideration. Bonuses may vary based on performance or tenure, so it's important to gather evidence such as past bonus payouts or company policies that highlight eligibility criteria. Including potential bonuses ensures that all forms of economic loss are accounted for.

While calculating these components, interim earnings cannot be overlooked. Any income earned from new employment during the litigation period typically offsets the total calculation of lost wages. For instance, if you secured another job after being wrongfully terminated, the difference between your old and new income needs to be deducted from your claim. This step ensures fairness and accuracy in the damage assessment.

Tax implications surrounding lost wages warrant careful examination. In general, the Internal Revenue Code specifies that compensatory damages, including lost wages, received due to non-physical injury claims, like wrongful termination, must be included in gross income. Consequently, these amounts are subject to income tax reporting requirements (Tax Implications of

Settlements and Judgments | Internal Revenue Service, n.d.). This necessitates an understanding of how settlements are structured and taxed.

Moreover, the reporting of such settlements is crucial. Typically, recipients and payors (employers issuing settlements) must comply with information return reporting requirements, such as issuing a Form 1099-MISC. This formality helps clarify tax obligations and supports compliance with IRS regulations.

Given the complexity of quantifying lost wages, consulting a forensic economic expert is often advisable. These specialists help filter through nuances such as anticipated raises, promotional opportunities, and unrealized earnings growth that might have occurred had the employment continued uninterrupted (Knowles, 2021). Their expertise ensures that no detail is overlooked, strengthening the validity of your calculations.

Additionally, settlement agreements might include clauses that define how payments should be characterized for tax purposes. These provisions can be beneficial, as they guide the determination of whether certain damages are taxable or excludable. However, clarity is imperative; if a settlement agreement lacks specificity, the IRS will likely interpret payments as taxable, using the intent of the payment issuer as a guideline (Tax Implications of Settlements and Judgments | Internal Revenue Service, n.d.).

It's equally important to recognize the variances between different types of damages within a settlement. While compensatory damages like lost wages are generally taxable, punitive damages, awarded to penalize defendants rather than to compensate for loss, are always subject to taxation. Understanding these distinctions prevents surprises during tax season and assists in negotiating settlements that align with your financial interests.

Addressing Emotional Distress Compensation

Emotional distress is a significant aspect of employment law disputes, often emerging from discriminatory practices and hostile work environments. It encompasses a range of psychological impacts, such as anxiety, depression, sleeplessness, and loss of enjoyment in life (admebman, 2020). Employment laws like Title VII of the Civil Rights Act allow for recovery of damages related to these emotional harms.

To quantify emotional distress legally, it's crucial to present compelling evidence in court. Documenting emotional distress effectively requires meticulous record-keeping. Plaintiffs can maintain journals detailing their emotional states and document any sleep disturbances or changes in mental health. Testimonies from friends and family members who witness the plaintiff's emotional state changes can also be invaluable.

Legal proceedings often demand robust proof of emotional harm. Expert testimonies play a pivotal role here. When higher damages are sought, courts may require testimony from psychologists or psychiatrists to substantiate claims (Bachman, 2022). A professional can provide an objective evaluation of the individual's mental health condition, linking it directly to workplace discrimination or harassment.

Analyzing precedent cases helps understand compensation trends for emotional distress. In Gross-Quattrone v. Mizdol, et al., the New Jersey case highlighted the potential need for disclosing personal information when pursuing such damages. The court examined the depth of emotional distress claimed by Judge Gross-Quattrone, assessing documentation from her medical records and personal testimonies to determine the validity of her claim (Bachman, 2022).

Precedent cases demonstrate that the severity and duration of emotional harm significantly influence compensation outcomes. Courts consider whether the individual sought medical treatment, which can help prove the legitimacy and extent of emotional distress. Hence, plaintiffs aiming for substantial compensation should prepare for detailed scrutiny into their personal and medical history.

Furthermore, psychological evaluations offer critical insights into the plaintiff's emotional status. These assessments detail conditions like depression or anxiety disorders, providing a concrete foundation for claiming emotional distress. Such evaluations, coupled with expert testimonies, strengthen the case for obtaining fair compensation by illustrating the direct impact of workplace misconduct on the individual's mental well-being.

Seeking emotional distress damages, however, involves weighing pros and cons. The process might expose plaintiffs to invasive inquiries about their personal lives. Employers may attempt to attribute the emotional harm to external factors unrelated to the workplace, probing past traumatic events or psychological history. This tactic aims to undermine the credibility of the emotional distress claim, making it essential for plaintiffs to provide clear causation between the employer's actions and their emotional suffering.

Given these complexities, navigating the legal landscape of emotional distress claims requires strategic preparation. Engaging qualified legal counsel familiar with employment law and emotional distress litigation is advisable. Legal experts help structure compelling arguments, ensuring all evidence effectively supports the claim.

Recovery of Legal Fees

Understanding the process and justification for recovering legal fees in employment cases can be both empowering and essential for those navigating these challenging waters. This section aims to break down the complexities surrounding legal fee recovery, providing clarity on how employees can reclaim their financial investment into justice after a favorable court ruling.

First, it's crucial to comprehend the provisions for awarding legal fees in employment-related lawsuits. These provisions often vary by jurisdiction, but generally, fee-shifting statutes exist to encourage individuals to pursue valid claims without bearing the prohibitive cost of litigation. For example, under laws like the Fair Labor Standards Act (FLSA) and certain state legislations, courts may order the losing party to pay the prevailing party's legal fees. In New York, Labor Law §198 (1-a) ensures that prevailing employees recover reasonable attorney's fees alongside other damages (Orser v Wholesale Fuel Distributors-CT, LLC, 2018).

Once you're aware of the existing provisions, the next step is formulating effective strategies to present a successful claim for attorney fees in court. The cornerstone of this strategy often lies in maintaining detailed, contemporaneous time records throughout the case. According to California law, this practice supports the lodestar method's application, which multiplies the hours reasonably spent by a reasonable hourly rate to compute the fee award (Maximizing Your Attorneys' Fees Recovery in the Trial Court Following a Successful FEHA Judgment, 2022). Additionally, presenting a well-organized fee petition that highlights the necessity and relevance of all billed hours to the successful claims can strengthen your case.

A key decision point involves choosing between contingency fee agreements and hourly billing in calculating recoverable costs. Contingency fees typically mean the attorney gets paid a percentage of the settlement or judgment awarded, incentivizing them to secure the highest possible amount for the client. On the other hand, hourly billing charges clients based on the time spent on their case. While both methods have merits, the choice often impacts the client's upfront costs and potential recovery. The lodestar calculation, commonly endorsed by courts, builds on the reasonable hours and rates rather than contingent percentages, offering a more predictable framework for awards (Hensley, supra, 461 U.S. at p. 440).

In practice, the judge's discretion plays a pivotal role in determining the award of legal fees. Factors such as the complexity of the case, the skill required, the outcome achieved, and even the conduct of the parties during litigation can influence this decision. Complex cases demanding significant legal expertise might justify higher fee awards. Judges also consider whether the result obtained was excellent compared to the relief sought; expansive victories often support full compensation through legal fees (Hensley, supra, 461 U.S. at p. 435).

The complexity of intertwining multiple legal claims further complicates matters when it comes to fee awards. Often, employment discrimination cases involve various causes of action based on similar facts. Courts recognize that separating time spent on fee-eligible and non-fee claims may not only be impractical but also unjust. Therefore, if claims are intertwined inextricably, the attorney should recover for all hours invested (Graciano v. Robinson Ford Sales, Inc. (2006) 144 Cal.App.4th 140, 159).

Moreover, handling cases where attorney fees exceed the plaintiff's monetary recovery requires a nuanced approach. Courts applying the lodestar method sometimes encounter situations where the legal fees surpass the awarded damages significantly. As misleading as this may seem, reducing fees solely based on disproportion could undermine statutory objectives, especially in civil rights cases. Judicious application of the lodestar principles ensures fair recompense for necessary and reasonable legal efforts, even if they dwarf the damage award (Vo v. Las Virgenes Muni Water Dist. (2000) 79 Cal.App.4th 440, 446).

Another layer to consider is the nuanced interplay between legal and common law claims. Often, claims under specific statutes come with fee-shifting provisions, whereas related common law claims do not. Nevertheless, when claims share a core factual basis or legal theories, courts may opt to award fees irrespective of success across all claims (Quaratino v. Tiffany & Co., 166 F.3d at 425).

Finally, transparency and honesty are paramount throughout this process. Fee requests deemed unreasonably inflated jeopardize the entire award, potentially prompting reductions or outright denials. Claimants must balance ambition with prudence, ensuring that each hour claimed aligns with the principles of reasonableness and necessity dictated by precedents like Serrano v. Unruh (Maximizing Your Attorneys' Fees Recovery in the Trial Court Following a Successful FEHA Judgment, 2022).

Closing Remarks

Navigating the path to job reinstatement and compensation after a favorable court ruling offers both a roadmap and a lesson in resilience for those affected by wrongful termination. This chapter has explored the detailed steps involved, from understanding labor laws to gathering crucial evidence. It underscores the necessity of aligning claims with legal standards to increase the likelihood of reinstatement, while also preparing for potential opposition from employers. The chapter provides insights into the importance of compiling comprehensive documentation and illustrates how mediation or legal counsel can help negotiate terms that align with both legal requirements and personal needs.

In addition to reinstatement, another key focus is on calculating lost wages and addressing emotional distress compensation. Understanding the financial implications of lost wages, including overtime and bonuses, becomes essential, especially when factoring in interim earnings and tax liabilities. Emotional distress damages represent a significant aspect of these cases, requiring clear evidence and expert testimonies to substantiate claims. As the journey progresses, navigating legal fees recovery helps demystify how individuals can reclaim their investment into seeking justice. By providing practical guidelines and a strategic approach, the chapter aims to empower not just wrongfully terminated employees, but also their families, healthcare workers, and legal allies in their pursuit of fairness and resolution.

Reference List

Bachman, E. (2022, February 22). New ruling examines emotional distress damages in employment cases – Bachman Law. Bachman Law. https://ebachmanlaw.com/new-ruling-examines-emotional-distress-damages-in-employment-cases/

Knowles, E. (2021, November 9). Calculating a Wrongful Termination Settlement - The Knowles Group. The Knowles Group. https://www.theknowlesgroup.org/blog/calculating-a-wrongful-termination-settlement/

Maximizing your attorneys' fees recovery in the trial court following a successful FEHA judgment. (2022). Advocatemagazine.com. https://www.advocatemagazine.com/article/2022-april/maximizing-your-attorneys-fees-recovery-in-the-trial-court-following-a-successful-feha-judgment

Orser v Wholesale Fuel Distributors-CT, LLC. (2018). Justia Law. https://law.justia.com/cases/new-york/other-courts/2018/2018-ny-slip-op-28436.html

Tax Implications of Settlements and Judgments | Internal Revenue Service. (n.d.). Www.irs.gov. https://www.irs.gov/government-entities/tax-implications-of-settlements-and-judgments

U.S. Department of Labor. (2024). Summary of the major laws of the department of labor. U.S. Department of Labor. https://www.dol.gov/general/aboutdol/majorlaws

U.S. Equal Employment Opportunity Commission. (2002, October 17). Enforcement Guidance on Reasonable Accommodation and Undue Hardship under the ADA | U.S. Equal Employment Opportunity Commission. Www.eeoc.gov. https://www.eeoc.gov/laws/guidance/enforcement-guidance-reasonable-accommodation-and-undue-hardship-under-ada

admebman. (2020, July 30). The ABC's of emotional distress damages in employment discrimination and retaliation cases – Bachman Law. Bachman Law. https://ebachmanlaw.com/the-abcs-of-emotional-distress-damages-in-employment-discrimination-and-retaliation-cases/

Chapter 10 How to Make Employers Pay for Their Unlawful Actions

Holding employers accountable for their unlawful actions, especially those taken during the COVID-19 pandemic, is crucial for safeguarding employee rights. Whether it's through challenging wrongful terminations or questioning the legality of strict mandates, employees are navigating a complex legal landscape to seek justice. With vaccination mandates and work-from-home debates taking center stage, the path to holding employers accountable involves understanding various legal avenues and adapting to ever-evolving regulations. Employees who faced job loss or pressure over mandates have found themselves looking to the legal system for remedies. This pursuit not only highlights the tension between workplace directives and personal freedoms but also underscores the ongoing battle many workers face in exercising their rights.

In this chapter, we'll explore the tactics employees can employ to address the overreach by employers, particularly focusing on the legal strategies available to them. You will learn how lawsuits have been used to challenge employer policies and what legal precedents have emerged from these challenges. The chapter delves into the nuances of regional differences in interpreting laws related to COVID-19 mandates, providing insights into how these have influenced court rulings across the country. Moreover, we'll discuss the ramifications these legal battles have on future employer policies, examining how recent court decisions are shaping the landscape of employment law. You'll gain an understanding of the roles various entities like OSHA and federal courts play in enforcing compliance and protecting worker rights, as well as the vital importance of documenting non-compliance and utilizing whistleblower protections effectively. Throughout, the chapter presents real-world examples and case studies that illustrate how employees have navigated these tumultuous waters to advocate for their rights.

The Growing Wave of Lawsuits Challenging COVID-19 Mandates

The COVID-19 pandemic has significantly altered workplace policies, prompting a wave of legal actions as employees challenge the mandates and restrictions imposed by employers. This surge in lawsuits focuses on vaccination mandates and refusals to allow remote work, often leading to disputes over individual rights versus employer obligations.

Employee-driven lawsuits have surged as vaccination mandates became more prevalent across various sectors. Many employees viewed these mandates as overreaching or infringing on personal freedom, leading them to seek legal recourse. Lawsuits like those involving large companies and federal contractors forced courts to tackle whether such mandates were lawful under existing labor laws. For instance, health-care workers in federally funded facilities faced ramifications from these mandates, which were sometimes upheld based on the broad authority given to agencies like the Centers for Medicare and Medicaid Services (CMS) (School, 2022).

Legal precedents have emerged from recent court rulings that highlight the complexity of addressing workplace policies during unprecedented times. The Occupational Safety and Health Administration's (OSHA) attempt to enforce a vax-or-test mandate was notably struck down due to perceived overreach, showcasing the delicate balance between public safety and legislative intent. These precedents are crucial for understanding how courts may interpret similar cases in the future, as seen when examining Title VII and ADA claims arising from COVID-19 protocols (Federal Courts in Wisconsin and Kentucky Issue Decisions in Favor of Employers Facing COVID-19–Related Legal Issues, 2023).

Regional differences play a significant role in how COVID-19-related employment disputes are handled. Courts in different states have varying interpretations of what constitutes an undue hardship for employers, particularly when accommodating religious beliefs or other exemptions. For example, federal trial courts in Wisconsin and Kentucky issued decisions favoring employers by dismissing claims related to vaccination requirements, interpreting objections not firmly rooted in religious doctrine as insufficient under Title VII (Federal Courts in Wisconsin and Kentucky Issue Decisions in Favor of Employers Facing COVID-19–Related Legal Issues, 2023).

These regional disparities reveal how localized legal cultures influence court rulings, creating a patchwork of decisions that affect both employers and employees nationwide. As courts continue to grapple with these issues, it's evident that state-specific legal landscapes will shape the outcomes of many COVID-19-related cases. This variability underscores the importance for employees and their legal representatives to consider regional legal climates when formulating cases.

The ripple effect of these lawsuits is profound, influencing current and future employer policies and workplace rights. Employers must now navigate a complex legal environment where employee challenges can prompt policy shifts. This situation forces companies to be cautious in implementing mandates to avoid potential litigation. The influence of lawsuits extends beyond individual cases, driving broader discussions about balancing workplace safety with personal freedoms. As businesses adjust, the conversation around what constitutes reasonable accommodations and privacy rights continues to evolve.

Moreover, the ongoing legal battles emphasize the need for clearer guidelines and legislation that address emerging workplace issues during public health crises. Policymakers might look to these legal outcomes to draft new laws that better define employer and employee responsibilities in situations where health and safety intersect with civil liberties.

Employees seeking legal guidance should closely monitor emerging trends in case law to understand their rights and the likelihood of success in challenging unlawful workplace actions. Similarly, employers aiming to formulate compliant workplace policies should pay attention to legal precedents and regional tendencies to anticipate potential pitfalls. As this landscape evolves, proactive engagement with legal experts who are well-versed in recent rulings becomes essential.

Accountability for Employers in the Future

The ongoing evolution of legal frameworks aimed at protecting employee rights in a post-COVID world is crucial for ensuring future employer accountability. As the pandemic reshapes workplace norms, governments and regulatory bodies have adapted legal policies to address challenges faced by employees. New regulations focus on safeguarding worker rights regarding health and safety, compensation, and privacy. The Occupational Safety and Health Administration (OSHA) plays a pivotal role, emphasizing updated guidelines that employers must follow. These regulations aim to protect employees from retaliation when they report violations or seek to enforce their rights. For example, OSHA's Whistleblower Protection Program enforces laws across various sectors, supporting workers who report hazards or legal breaches (COVID-19 - Regulations | Occupational Safety and Health Administration, 2019). This evolving framework reflects the need to adapt to new paradigms where telework, hybrid models, and enhanced safety measures become standard.

Government agencies such as OSHA are instrumental in enforcing compliance with new workplace safety standards. Throughout the pandemic, these agencies have been tasked with adapting oversight mechanisms to ensure employers adhere to updated health directives and provide safe working environments. This involves routine inspections and evaluations to verify compliance with health protocols, including proper sanitation, physical distancing, and provision of personal protective equipment (PPE). Agencies impose fines and penalties on organizations that fail to meet these standards, ensuring employers take proactive measures to maintain workplace safety. The emphasis on government intervention underscores the importance of having an external check on employer practices, minimizing the risk of exploitation or negligence.

Employers who fail to adapt to updated legal requirements face significant repercussions. Failure to comply with safety regulations not only results in financial penalties but also damages an organization's reputation. In severe cases, non-compliance can lead to business closures or legal action from employees. For instance, inadequate response to COVID-19 cases or failure to disclose exposure to employees might result in lawsuits or workplace disruptions. Repercussions extend beyond immediate penalties; they can affect long-term viability as consumers and prospective employees increasingly prioritize ethical and responsible companies. Employers must remain vigilant and responsive to evolving regulations to avoid adverse outcomes.

To ensure sustained accountability from their organizations, employees can employ several strategies. Understanding their rights under current laws is paramount. Workers should familiarize themselves with OSHA regulations and relevant employment laws tailored to their industry and location. Empowerment through knowledge enables employees to recognize violations and act accordingly. Documenting incidents of non-compliance is a valuable tool for substantiating claims, especially in legal contexts. Communication within the workforce can amplify individual concerns, leading to collective action when necessary. Employees should consider forming or joining unions, which can provide structured support for negotiating better terms and holding employers accountable.

Another vital strategy involves utilizing whistleblower protections effectively. By reporting unsafe or unlawful practices, employees not only protect their personal interests but contribute to broader organizational accountability. It is crucial to file complaints promptly, ensuring they fall within statutory timeframes to avoid dismissal due to procedural issues. Furthermore, employees should leverage digital platforms and social media responsibly to raise awareness about unjust practices while maintaining anonymity and adhering to company policies. This can increase public scrutiny and pressure organizations to rectify issues swiftly.

Importance of Legal Victories for Personal Freedom and Bodily Autonomy

The significance of courtroom victories in reinforcing individual liberties is profound. Court decisions, especially those borne out of contentious issues such as workplace mandates during the COVID-19 pandemic, have a lasting impact on personal freedoms and set the stage for future legal battles concerning bodily autonomy at work.

Judicial decisions often serve as a double-edged sword in the realm of personal freedoms. On the one hand, they have the power to reinforce liberties, upholding rights and setting new standards for what is legally permissible. On the other hand, they can constrain freedoms, depending on the outcomes and interpretations of the law. As seen in history, landmark cases shape our understanding and implementation of civil liberties. For instance, the period from the mid-20th century saw the Supreme Court making significant strides in defending individual rights, contrasting sharply with its earlier rulings that favored business and elite interests (Gabriella Sanchez, 2024).

Precedent-setting cases play a pivotal role in shaping future legal landscapes. When courts decide on complex issues like bodily autonomy in the workplace, these decisions become benchmarks for subsequent claims. A notable example is the evolution of equal protection under the law, which, according to The Court, the Constitution, and the Culture of Freedom source, has been interpreted progressively by the Supreme Court to accommodate broader notions of freedom and equality (The Court, the Constitution, and the Culture of Freedom, n.d.). These precedents inform how similar cases are judged, creating a continuum of legal reasoning that expands or contracts the boundaries of personal rights.

Furthermore, when courts uphold or breach personal rights, the societal implications are vast. Upholding rights can lead to wider acceptance and integration of these freedoms into the fabric of society, while breaching them could engender public dissent and necessitate legislative reforms. The Supreme Court's role here, acting as the arbiter of constitutional freedoms, influences societal norms and expectations. Past rulings, especially those concerning civil rights, women's rights, and more recently, issues like same-sex marriage, demonstrate the court's influence in driving or stalling social progress (Gabriella Sanchez, 2024).

The role of successful litigants in employment law cannot be understated. They often emerge as symbols of resistance and change, inspiring others to challenge unjust policies. Their victories not only bring about legal redress but also motivate legislators and employers to re-evaluate existing practices and policies. These litigants, through their tenacity and courage, catalyze necessary changes in the employment law landscape, pushing it towards greater fairness and equity.

Broader Impact of Legal Challenges on Employment Practices

In the rapidly evolving landscape of employment law, high-profile legal challenges have had significant ripple effects on workplace norms and practices. These changes are not just theoretical; they shape the daily experiences of employees and employers alike. One of the most notable impacts has been the shift in corporate policy-making influenced by these legal battles.

In recent years, legal actions have increasingly driven corporations to reassess their internal policies, particularly those related to employee rights and workplace safety. A prominent example of this can be seen through lawsuits challenging COVID-19 vaccine mandates. These legal challenges have forced companies to reconsider how they balance public health concerns with individual freedoms. As corporations navigate these complex issues, many have opted to revise their policies to both protect their workforce and adhere to legal standards, often resulting in more flexible remote work arrangements or alternative compliance measures for employees unable or unwilling to comply with certain mandates.

This balancing act between employee demands and business interests is a constantly shifting dynamic, largely shaped by the outcomes of recent court cases. Companies are finding themselves walking a tightrope—striving to maintain productivity and profitability while addressing the legal rights and concerns of their workforce. Legal precedents established through litigation have compelled businesses to prioritize transparency and dialogue with employees, creating a more collaborative approach to policy development. This new paradigm requires employers to be more attuned to the needs of their employees, thereby fostering environments where communication and compromise become essential elements of everyday operations.

The influence of legal outcomes on workplace norms is further underscored by case studies highlighting tangible changes in employer-employee dynamics due to litigation. For instance, several lawsuits targeting unfair dismissal during pandemic-related furloughs and layoffs have spotlighted the need for clearer communication and procedural fairness within organizations. Companies implicated in such lawsuits have often emerged with revamped grievance procedures and more detailed employment contracts that protect both parties' interests.

One illustrative case is the lawsuit against a major retail corporation accused of unjustly terminating workers who refused COVID-19 vaccinations. The legal proceedings pressured the company to institute broader accommodation policies, ultimately leading to a substantial overhaul of its employment practices. The repercussions of this litigation extended beyond the immediate parties involved, setting a standard for other organizations grappling with similar issues. As these cases illustrate, litigation does not merely resolve disputes but catalyzes widespread systemic change, influencing how businesses operate long after the courtroom doors close.

Forecasting future trends in employment law reform reveals that current legal debates will likely continue to shape how workplaces function. Recent lawsuits serve as harbingers of potential regulatory shifts, indicating areas where current legislation may fall short. For example, as courts hear more cases concerning remote work agreements and digital privacy, legislative bodies might consider instituting comprehensive laws that better define employers' obligations and employees' rights in virtual work settings.

Moreover, sector-specific regulations could emerge in response to legal precedents set by ongoing litigation. Industries heavily impacted by the pandemic, such as healthcare and education, may see more tailored laws designed to address unique challenges faced by their workforce. These reforms could include enhanced protections for whistleblowers, stricter enforcement of workplace safety standards, and clearer guidelines for accommodating employees with varying health concerns.

In this context, it is crucial for businesses to remain proactive in adapting to potential legal changes. Staying informed about ongoing legal cases and participating in industry discussions can help organizations anticipate regulatory shifts and prepare accordingly. As the legal landscape evolves, companies willing to embrace change and implement preventive measures will be better positioned to foster resilient, compliant workplaces.

Insights and Implications

The chapter has explored how employees are navigating the complexities of holding employers accountable for unlawful acts during COVID-19 mandates, emphasizing the role of lawsuits in shaping workplace dynamics. As we've seen through various court cases, legal challenges against vaccination mandates and other COVID-related policies have sparked broad discussions around personal freedoms, workplace safety, and employer obligations. This has highlighted the delicate balance between public health measures and individual rights, often resulting in new precedents that influence future legal interpretations. It's crucial for individuals, especially those wrongfully terminated or seeking legal guidance, to stay informed on these trends as they consider their options.

Looking ahead, it's evident that the landscape of labor laws will continue to evolve as both employees and employers seek clarity on their rights and responsibilities. Regulatory bodies like OSHA are integral to this process, enforcing updated guidelines and ensuring compliance with safety standards. For healthcare workers, first responders, and others directly affected by these mandates, understanding regulatory changes and potential legal recourses is vital. Similarly, legal advocates and concerned citizens should keep abreast of emerging case law to effectively champion bodily autonomy and protect constitutional rights. Ultimately, proactive engagement with legal experts and an awareness of evolving legal frameworks are essential for navigating the post-COVID workplace environment effectively.

Reference List

Business Ethics Cases - Markkula Center for Applied Ethics. (n.d.). Www.scu.edu. https://www.scu.edu/ethics/focus-areas/business-ethics/resources/cases/

COVID-19 - Regulations | Occupational Safety and Health Administration. (2019). Osha.gov. http://www.osha.gov/coronavirus/standards

Federal Courts in Wisconsin and Kentucky Issue Decisions in Favor of Employers Facing COVID-19–Related Legal Issues. (2023, October 16). Ogletree. https://ogletree.com/insights-resources/blog-posts/federal-courts-in-wisconsin-and-kentucky-issue-decisions-in-favor-of-employers-facing-covid-19-related-legal-issues/

Gabriella Sanchez. (2024, October 7). Landmark Supreme Court Cases. Brennan Center for Justice. https://www.brennancenter.org/our-work/research-reports/landmark-supreme-court-cases

School, S. L. (2022, January 20). A Look at the Supreme Court Ruling on Vaccination Mandates. Stanford Law School. https://law.stanford.edu/2022/01/20/a-look-at-the-supreme-court-ruling-on-vaccination-mandates/

Sanction Scanner. (2024, September 27). Impacts of Government Regulations on Businesses - Sanction Scanner. Sanctionscanner.com. https://www.sanctionscanner.com/blog/impacts-of-government-regulations-on-businesses-312

The Court, the Constitution, and the Culture of Freedom. (n.d.). Hoover Institution. https://www.hoover.org/research/court-constitution-and-culture-freedom

johnk. (2020, August 31). Covid-19 Workplace Lawyers. Blair & Ramirez LLP. https://www.blairramirezlaw.com/covid-19-workplace-lawyers

Chapter 11: How to Make Employers Pay for Their Unlawful Actions

The wrongful termination of employees under illegal COVID-19 mandates has led to a wave of lawsuits against employers who disregarded employee rights. Those who were fired for refusing the jab have legal grounds to demand compensation for financial loss, emotional distress, and punitive damages. In this chapter, we will explore strategic ways to pressure employers into settlements, how to maximize compensation, and why lawsuits will deter future employer misconduct.

Strategies to Pressure Employers into Settlements

1. Building a Strong Case Before Filing a Lawsuit

Employers are more likely to settle if they know you have an airtight case. To strengthen your claim:

- **Collect Evidence:** Gather termination notices, emails, performance records, employee handbooks, and any communication related to vaccine policies.
- **Find Witnesses:** If coworkers faced similar terminations, they can provide testimony or join a class-action suit.
- **Document Financial Losses:** Keep track of lost wages, job search expenses, and any medical costs related to stress or emotional harm.
- **Consult a Lawyer:** Employment attorneys can assess your case and determine the best legal strategy.

2. File a Formal Complaint Before Suing

In some cases, an official complaint can push an employer to negotiate a settlement before a lawsuit begins.

- **File with the EEOC:** If discrimination played a role in your firing, an EEOC (Equal Employment Opportunity Commission) complaint can be filed.

- **State Labor Boards:** Many states have labor commissions that investigate wrongful terminations.
- **Send a Demand Letter:** Before suing, have a lawyer draft a formal letter demanding compensation and outlining potential legal action.

3. Public Pressure and Media Exposure

No employer wants bad press. If your wrongful termination was particularly egregious, consider:

- **Contacting Journalists:** Local or national media outlets may be interested in covering cases where employees were fired over unlawful mandates.
- **Social Media Awareness:** Sharing your story (without defamation) can build public support and force employers to respond.
- **Class-Action Lawsuits:** If multiple employees were fired under similar circumstances, a class-action lawsuit can gain momentum and force settlements.

How to Demand Back Pay, Emotional Distress Compensation, and Punitive Damages

Once you've taken the initial legal steps, you should seek full compensation for the damages suffered.

1. Back Pay and Future Earnings

Employers who wrongfully terminated workers can be ordered to compensate for:

- **Lost Wages:** All income lost since the termination date.
- **Lost Benefits:** If health insurance, 401(k) contributions, or bonuses were affected.
- **Reinstatement or Equivalent Compensation:** Courts may force an employer to rehire you or pay out future earnings.

2. Emotional Distress Compensation

Being fired unjustly causes emotional and psychological harm. You may be entitled to:

- **Compensation for Anxiety and Depression:** If you experienced significant stress, sleep disorders, or other emotional struggles due to wrongful termination.
- **Therapy or Counseling Costs:** Employers may be required to cover mental health expenses incurred due to their unlawful actions.
- **Impact on Family Stability:** If the termination caused a loss of home, schooling issues for children, or marital problems, these can be considered in damages.

3. Punitive Damages

Punitive damages are awarded to **punish** an employer for willful misconduct and to deter future violations. These are typically granted when:

- The employer acted with **malice** or **reckless disregard** for employee rights.
- Vaccine mandates were enforced **without proper exemption procedures**.
- The employer knowingly violated labor laws and **refused to settle fairly**.

Why More Lawsuits Mean Fewer Employer Abuses in the Future

Every successful lawsuit sets a legal precedent that helps others fight back against employer overreach. By holding employers accountable:

1. Strengthening Employee Rights

Winning lawsuits establish clear **legal boundaries** on vaccine mandates and workplace policies. Future employers will think twice before unlawfully firing employees.

2. Forcing Policy Changes

Major corporations and institutions often modify their policies **after losing lawsuits**. For example:

- **Medical and Religious Exemptions Will Be Taken More Seriously.**
- **Employment Contracts Will Be Clearer Regarding Mandates.**
- **Wrongful Termination Cases Will Deter Future Firings.**

3. Financial Consequences for Employers

- Companies that face **multiple lawsuits** will see increased insurance rates, reduced investor confidence, and reputational damage.
- When enough lawsuits are filed, **corporate vaccine mandates may be permanently dismantled**.

Final Thoughts

Employers who wrongfully terminated workers for refusing COVID-19 vaccination **must be held accountable**. Through strategic legal action, employees can secure financial justice, force corporate change, and prevent future abuses. Filing lawsuits and seeking settlements are not just personal victories—they are critical steps toward restoring employee rights across the workforce.

Chapter 12 Navigating Legal Challenges Around Vaccine-Related Terminations

Navigating the complex world of legal challenges around vaccine-related terminations is a daunting task faced by many today. With mandates becoming more widespread and deeply affecting various sectors, individuals find themselves at the crossroads of personal choice and professional obligations. This chapter delves into these challenging scenarios, aiming to equip readers with the knowledge needed to protect their rights effectively. While vaccine mandates have sparked diverse opinions and contentious debates across workplaces, understanding how to confront termination issues requires careful consideration and informed decision-making.

In this chapter, you'll discover valuable insights into crafting an impactful demand letter to your former employer. Learn how to structure your communication so that it not only addresses grievances but also lays a solid foundation for any potential legal proceedings. The importance of clarity, professionalism, and documentation will be highlighted, guiding you on how to present a compelling case right from the start. Additionally, the chapter explores the avenues available for finding the right legal representation in vaccine-related terminations. By evaluating a lawyer's expertise specifically within this niche area, you can significantly improve your chances of securing effective advocacy.

Moreover, the chapter provides an overview of recent pivotal court decisions shaping the current landscape of vaccine mandate-related employment disputes. These cases underscore the intricate relationship between public health initiatives and individual employment rights, offering lessons that would benefit anyone navigating this new terrain. You'll also find strategies tailored to strengthen your case, from gathering relevant evidence to building a comprehensive personal narrative that aligns with legal standards. Successful navigation of these challenges often depends on how well-prepared you are and how effectively you can anticipate the opposition's arguments.

For those feeling overwhelmed by the potential for legal battles, this chapter serves as both a guide and a resource. It encourages readers to take proactive measures in asserting their rights while maintaining a respectful dialogue with employers. Emphasizing the need for adaptability, it ensures you're better prepared to handle evolving laws and regulations surrounding vaccine mandates. As these discussions unfold, this chapter stands as a critical companion, supporting individuals every step of the way towards achieving fair outcomes in these turbulent times.

Writing a Demand Letter to Your Former Employer

One of the pivotal steps for those facing termination due to vaccine mandates is writing an effective demand letter. A demand letter serves as a formal request to address grievances and seek resolution without immediately resorting to litigation. Its purpose extends beyond merely asking for redress; it plays a crucial role in documenting your attempts to resolve disputes amicably. This step can be particularly significant if you later choose to pursue legal action, as it demonstrates a willingness to settle matters outside of court, potentially favoring your position under pre-litigation requirements (uclseomanager, 2025).

Structuring a well-organized demand letter is essential to convey seriousness and clarity. Begin with a clear heading that includes your name, contact details, and the date. Address the letter to the appropriate party, ensuring you include their full name and position if applicable. The introduction should succinctly outline the purpose of your letter, referencing the employment situation that led to termination. Be explicit about why you're writing, such as outlining dissatisfaction with the circumstances or requesting specific remedies.

The body of the demand letter is where you delve into details. Provide a chronological account of events leading to termination, citing relevant facts and dates. Highlight key incidents that demonstrate either noncompliance with legal standards or procedural irregularities in your dismissal process. It's vital to reference any legal frameworks or contractual obligations breached by the employer. Specify what remedy you are seeking clearly—whether it's reinstatement, financial compensation, or another form of redress. Being precise about your demands not only solidifies your seriousness but also guides the recipient towards addressing your concerns appropriately (Daniel H. Weberman, 2024).

Conclude your demand letter by setting a reasonable deadline for the recipient to respond or act. Outlining consequences for non-compliance, such as potential legal proceedings, adds weight to your demands and encourages timely engagement from the opposite party. However, ensure that your tone remains professional throughout. While it might be tempting to express frustration or anger, maintaining a respectful tone enhances your credibility and helps preserve a constructive dialogue. Avoid aggressive language; instead, use firm yet polite phrasing to assert your rights and the resolution you expect.

Writing with clarity is equally important—avoid jargon or overly technical language that could confuse the recipient. Simplicity aids in comprehension and ensures your message is not lost in translation. Supplement your claims with supporting documentation like employment contracts, termination notices, or email correspondences to bolster your arguments. These add legitimacy to your demands, demonstrating preparedness and thoroughness to the reader (uclseomanager, 2025).

While a guideline for writing a demand letter isn't always necessary, providing one can help ensure clarity throughout your communication. Consider referring to resources like sample legal letters and documents as useful tools for structuring your document effectively. Such examples can serve as templates to guide individuals unfamiliar with legal writing through the process more smoothly.

Maintaining professionalism in your demand letter cannot be understated. Adopt a tone that balances assertiveness with diplomacy. Remember, the recipient's perception of your demeanor can influence their response. By presenting yourself as reasonable and open to dialogue, you're more likely to foster a cooperative atmosphere conducive to resolving disputes. Demonstrating empathy towards the recipient's perspective, even as you assert your rights, can further pave the way for constructive negotiations and settlement talks (Daniel H. Weberman, 2024).

Common pitfalls to avoid in drafting a demand letter include omitting critical information like exact demands or deadlines. Vagueness weakens the letter's impact and may lead to misinterpretation or dismissal. Neglecting legal formalities, such as sending the letter via certified mail, can undermine its enforceability. To circumvent these mistakes, carefully review all elements of your draft before dispatching it. Seek input from trusted advisors or legal professionals to refine your document, ensuring it aligns with your objectives and adheres to legal standards.

Finding Legal Representation

When facing termination due to vaccine mandates, it's crucial for individuals to find the right legal representation to ensure their rights are protected. This subpoint aims to guide readers in selecting suitable legal representation specifically experienced in handling vaccine-related termination cases.

Firstly, identifying law firms that specialize in employment law and have a proven track record with vaccine-related terminations is essential. Not all law firms have the required experience in this niche area. Individuals should look for firms that explicitly list wrongful terminations, including those related to vaccine refusal, as part of their practice areas. According to Siri & Glimstad LLP, specializing in COVID-19 related employment issues, such specificity in practice enables lawyers to stay updated on the latest legal developments and strategies in this evolving field (COVID-19 Vaccine Termination - Siri & Glimstad LLP, 2024).

An initial consultation plays a pivotal role in determining the suitability of a potential lawyer or firm. During this first meeting, clients should assess whether the lawyer has a clear understanding of employment law nuances concerning vaccine mandates. Important questions to ask include: What is your experience with vaccine mandate cases? How successful have you been in similar cases? Can you outline your approach to my situation? The consultation is not only about the lawyer evaluating your case but also about you assessing the lawyer's expertise and compatibility with your needs.

Evaluating a lawyer's credentials involves looking beyond their specialization in employment law. It's beneficial to examine their educational background, years of experience, and any certifications in related legal fields. Additionally, it's wise to consider their case success rates. A lawyer with a higher percentage of wins in similar cases could be more adept at navigating the complexities of vaccine-related terminations. Client reviews can serve as another vital resource. Websites and forums where previous clients share their experiences can provide insight into the lawyer's professionalism, communication skills, and overall effectiveness. Look for consistent positive feedback regarding the lawyer's ability to handle challenging cases and achieve favorable outcomes.

Understanding fee structures is also critical in choosing legal representation. Lawyers typically charge by the hour, work on contingency, or use a hybrid model combining both methods. In vaccine-related termination cases, a contingency fee arrangement might be appealing because it implies that the lawyer only gets paid if you win your case. However, transparency in financial agreements is paramount, ensuring there are no hidden fees or unexpected charges. During the initial consultation, request a detailed breakdown of the expected costs. Inquire about any additional expenses outside of the standard attorney fees, such as court filing fees or costs associated with gathering evidence.

Transparency in these agreements builds trust and avoids potential conflicts over financial matters later on. Some law firms may offer flexible payment plans or reduced fees for clients with limited financial resources, which is worth exploring during your discussions.

Navigating legal challenges around vaccine-related terminations requires careful consideration and informed decision-making. By identifying specialized law firms, conducting thorough initial consultations, evaluating credentials and success rates, and understanding fee structures, individuals can increase their chances of securing effective legal representation tailored to their specific needs.

Understanding Key Court Decisions

Legal precedents surrounding vaccine mandates and related terminations have become focal points in understanding the intricate relationship between public health initiatives and employment rights. This discourse is increasingly relevant as individuals and employers navigate the complexities imposed by the unprecedented challenge of COVID-19.

One pivotal Supreme Court case that shaped the legal landscape around vaccine mandates is the recent ruling on the Biden administration's attempt to enforce vaccination or regular testing for employees at businesses with over 100 workers. In this instance, the court blocked the Occupational Safety and Health Administration (OSHA) emergency rule affecting millions. The decision underscored the judicial interpretation where the power granted by Congress to OSHA was deemed insufficient for enforcing such broad mandates. This ruling highlighted the balance courts must strike between agency authority and legislative intent, illustrating the limitations placed on federal bodies regulating workplace safety under specific statutory scopes (School, 2022).

In contrast, the court upheld a mandate from the Centers for Medicare and Medicaid Services requiring vaccinations for healthcare workers at federally funded facilities. This decision reflected a nuanced understanding of different regulatory environments and showcased the court's willingness to recognize the broader public health objectives justifying the mandate. Through this lens, it is evident that legal interpretations are not uniform but vary significantly based on the context in which mandates are applied (School, 2022).

The discrepancies seen in these judicial interpretations across jurisdictions further complicate the legal framework that both employees and employers must navigate. In some states, courts have shown more leniency towards vaccine mandates, often prioritizing public health concerns over individual objections. For instance, historical cases like Jacobson v. Massachusetts have long supported the notion that state-imposed vaccine mandates do not violate constitutional rights if they are reasonable and necessary for public health. However, the balancing act between collective safety and individual liberties remains a contentious issue, with contemporary courts occasionally deviating from past precedents depending on the specifics of each case (Rothstein et al., 2021).

These decisions also ripple out to impact employee rights and employer responsibilities, setting precedents that shape workplace policies. Employers now face heightened scrutiny regarding their immunization policies' legality and implementation. They must carefully consider offering exemptions and understanding the potential for legal challenges if these accommodations appear insufficient in addressing employees' medical or religious concerns. As a result, many employers opt to consult legal experts when tailoring their policies to ensure alignment with both federal guidance and the fluctuating state-level regulations (Rothstein et al., 2021).

Recent developments in vaccination mandates are deeply intertwined with broader public health and employment policies. Initiatives taken by employers are often reflective of overarching strategies aimed at curbing the pandemic, aiming to assuage economic setbacks while safeguarding workplace health. It presents a dichotomy where achieving herd immunity through workplace mandates may clash with personal freedoms, highlighting the ongoing debate about the ethics and effectiveness of such measures. Despite their intentions, rigid enforcement without room for flexibility can exacerbate resistance among employees who feel coerced, potentially leading to increased legal disputes.

Moreover, the provisions surrounding vaccine mandates often intersect with existing labor laws, challenging traditional notions of bodily autonomy versus communal welfare. Employment attorneys and legal advocates play a crucial role here, acting as intermediaries who mediate between preserving individual rights and meeting public safety imperatives. These cases are emblematic of broader social debates, forcing stakeholders at every level—from policymakers to companies—to continually evaluate and adjust their approaches in response to evolving legal landscapes.

Strategies to Strengthen Your Case

Equipping individuals with the necessary tools to navigate legal challenges surrounding vaccine-related terminations is crucial in such uncertain times. This section aims to provide practical strategies for building a robust legal case, especially for those who find themselves in this unenviable position.

To begin with, the foundation of any strong legal case lies in collecting and organizing all relevant documents. This includes employment contracts and termination notices, which are critical in establishing the terms of your employment and the reasons behind your termination. It's essential to thoroughly review these documents to understand your rights as outlined by your employer. For example, an employment contract might include clauses about mandatory health requirements that must be met, or it might detail conditions under which termination could occur. Having these documents well-organized not only aids in clarity but also ensures that you have prompt access when needed for legal consultations or court proceedings (Practical Law, 2018).

Next, gathering supportive evidence to bolster your claims is another crucial step. It's important to collect communications with your employer, such as emails or written correspondences, that discuss your stance on vaccine mandates. These records can demonstrate whether there was a dialogue or an attempt to address concerns before termination occurred. Additionally, for those with medical conditions, obtaining medical records that may highlight contraindications for certain vaccines is vital. These records can serve as factual evidence that could potentially justify refusal based on legitimate health grounds. The more comprehensive your evidence is, the stronger your case will be.

Crafting a personal narrative is equally important; this narrative should highlight key facts and aim to align closely with legal standards. Your story should succinctly lay out the sequence of events leading up to the termination. Include details like the communication timeline between you and your employer, actions taken following mandate announcements, and any attempts made for exemption requests. Remember, your narrative is not just a recounting of events but a strategic tool designed to invoke empathy and understanding while adhering to legal frameworks. This segment of your preparation humanizes your case and provides context beyond mere documentation.

Furthermore, collaborating effectively with legal counsel is paramount. An attorney experienced in employment law, particularly with cases involving vaccine mandates, can offer significant insights into refining your legal arguments. They can assist in crafting a compelling narrative that anticipates potential counterarguments from the opposing side. Together with your lawyer, you'll need to prepare to respond to common defenses that employers may present, such as arguments regarding workplace safety and regulatory compliance.

Anticipating counterarguments involves understanding the defenses your employer might raise and being ready with rebuttals. This collaborative approach ensures that you're not just reacting to the other side's case but proactively shaping your defense with foresight and strategy. Lawyers will often suggest mock trial sessions or role-playing exercises to help you practice articulating your narrative and addressing questions under pressure.

An organized approach in managing your case is indispensable. As emphasized in case management tips, maintaining a checklist can help ensure that no tasks or pieces of evidence are overlooked (Tips for Effective Case Management, n.d.). A structured list serves as both a roadmap and a progress tracker, keeping track of what has been accomplished and what remains pending. This organizational tool becomes particularly valuable when timelines are tight or in situations requiring swift action.

Finally, while preparing for legal battles, it's important to keep informed about the evolving legislative environment concerning vaccine mandates. Laws and regulations in this area may change rapidly, influenced by public health developments and legal precedents. Staying updated will equip you to adapt your strategies and reinforce your case as needed.

Concluding Thoughts

In navigating the challenges of vaccine-related terminations, this chapter equips individuals with practical steps to protect their rights and seek resolution. Writing a demand letter to your former employer emerges as a critical tool, serving both as a formal grievance and a potential precursor to legal action. By ensuring proper structure and clarity, this letter not only documents disputes amicably but also strengthens any subsequent legal case by demonstrating a willingness to resolve matters outside of court. Equally important is finding specialized legal representation, which involves assessing law firms experienced in handling vaccine-related terminations. With the right lawyer, individuals can better navigate the complexities of employment law, enhancing their chances of a favorable outcome.

Understanding key court decisions and building a strong case become equally crucial. Legal precedents surrounding vaccine mandates reveal the ongoing tension between public health initiatives and employment rights, highlighting how legal interpretations vary based on context. This underscores the necessity for thorough documentation and strategic narrative crafting when strengthening an individual's case against wrongful termination. Collaborating effectively with legal counsel, preparing for counterarguments, and maintaining organized case management ensure that no detail is overlooked. Ultimately, staying informed about evolving regulations remains vital in adapting strategies, empowering individuals to protect their rights and find justice amidst these challenging circumstances.

Reference List

COVID-19 Vaccine Termination - Siri & Glimstad LLP. (2024, January 25). Siri & Glimstad LLP. https://doi.org/10010399/et-divi-dynamic-tb-1458-tb-882-10010399-late

COVID-19 Employment Defense Attorneys| PBW Law. (2023, September 14). Pearlman, Brown & Wax. https://www.pbw-law.com/areas-of-law/covid-19-employment-defense/

Daniel H. Weberman. (2024). Dhweberman.com. https://www.dhweberman.com/post/how-to-write-an-effective-demand-letter

Practical Law. (2018). @Westlaw1. https://legal.thomsonreuters.com/en/products/practical-law

Rothstein, M. A., Parmet, W. E., & Reiss, D. R. (2021, February 4). Employer-Mandated Vaccination for COVID-19. American Journal of Public Health. https://doi.org/10.2105/ajph.2020.306166

School, S. L. (2022, January 20). A Look at the Supreme Court Ruling on Vaccination Mandates. Stanford Law School. https://law.stanford.edu/2022/01/20/a-look-at-the-supreme-court-ruling-on-vaccination-mandates/

Tips for effective case management. (n.d.). Www.wolterskluwer.com. https://www.wolterskluwer.com/en-gb/expert-insights/effective-case-management-tips

uclseomanager. (2025, January 31). Crafting an Effective Demand Letter: A Step-by-Step Guide. Hartley Law Firm. https://hartleylawtx.com/blog/crafting-an-effective-demand-letter/

Conclusion

In recent years, the global landscape has shifted dramatically in response to the COVID-19 pandemic, impacting countless lives and reshaping societal norms. For many employees, especially those who stood firm against vaccination mandates, the repercussions have been particularly severe. They faced wrongful terminations, job loss apprehensions, and overwhelming uncertainty. The journey has been fraught with challenges, but it is crucial to recognize that this struggle transcends personal battles—it underscores a broader fight for rights, justice, and societal accountability.

The unprecedented nature of the pandemic brought with it an array of complex legal dynamics that were previously uncharted territory. As industries adapted to rapidly changing health guidelines, individuals found themselves at the intersection of personal choice and professional risk. Those who opposed the COVID-19 vaccine faced not just potential health concerns but also economic pressures, ethical dilemmas, and social stigmatization. Among these individuals are healthcare workers—nurses, doctors, and hospital staff—who, despite being on the frontline, were abruptly sidelined for their choices. Similarly, first responders like police officers and firefighters, often celebrated as heroes, found themselves discharged for non-compliance with vaccination mandates.

This book serves as both a guide and a beacon of hope for those affected. With new legal rulings coming to light, such as evidence presented by prominent figures like RFK Jr., there's renewed optimism. These developments are reshaping the legal narrative, offering terminated employees an opportunity to reassess their circumstances and consider legal recourse. Importantly, recent moves toward reinstating military personnel who faced similar fates underscore the shifting tides, suggesting a growing acknowledgment of past injustices.

For the wrongfully terminated, knowledge is power. This book equips former employees with the necessary tools to challenge their dismissals. It breaks down complex legal jargon into accessible language, ensuring that readers feel empowered rather than overwhelmed. From understanding your rights under labor laws to strategically navigating potential lawsuits, the insights provided are invaluable. If you've found yourself in this predicament, remember: you're not alone, and your voice matters.

Legal and labor rights advocates play a pivotal role in this narrative. Employment attorneys championing these causes bring expertise and passion, supporting those unjustly treated. Their efforts, combined with activists promoting bodily autonomy and medical freedom, have sparked a broader societal discussion about governmental authority and individual rights. The discourse around vaccine mandates isn't just a question of public health; it's intertwined with constitutional debates and deeply held convictions about personal freedom.

Moreover, political landscapes have been significantly influenced. Conservatives, libertarians, and independents argue that the mandates represent government overreach—a stance that resonates with many across the nation. For them, the issue extends beyond mere employment; it touches the core of what it means to live freely under a democratic system. The political implications are profound, yet they share a common goal with terminated employees: the pursuit of justice and reparation.

This book also acknowledges the secondary audiences whose lives were upended by these decisions. Families of terminated employees have borne the brunt of financial hardships, facing uncertainty and emotional strain. Their struggles are tangible reminders of the real-life consequences lockdowns and mandates have wrought upon ordinary citizens. Vaccine-injured individuals, too, share parallel experiences. Initially compliant out of necessity or coercion, they now navigate unforeseen health challenges, advocating for change from personal conviction.

Whistleblowers and investigative researchers are integral in revealing the multifaceted issues surrounding COVID-19 mandates. Their exposure of flawed policies and questionable science has highlighted the importance of transparency and accountability. Through their courage, they've paved the way for informed discussions, helping society understand the layered complexities behind decisions that affected millions.

As we approach a new chapter, reflection becomes essential. While the scars of wrongful termination and enforced compliance remain fresh, there is solace in knowing that perseverance can lead to progress. Each step taken—from filing a lawsuit to advocating for policy change—contributes to a larger movement demanding integrity and fairness.

Looking ahead, the lessons learned during this period hold transformative potential. By challenging wrongful practices, individuals not only seek justice for themselves but also lay down markers for future generations. It's an opportunity to redefine workplace ethics, ensuring respect for individual choices while maintaining collective safety.

In closing, let this book be a reminder that every challenge faced is shared. It stands testament to the strength and resilience inherent in those who dared to stand against prevailing currents. Whether you're pursuing legal action, engaging in advocacy, or simply seeking to understand your situation better, remember that change is possible—and your actions contribute to a greater call for equity and respect.

Ultimately, the fight against wrongful termination rooted in unjust mandates is part of a broader quest for truth, fairness, and dignity. Together, with resolve and righteousness, we can shape a more just world.

The Legal Lie—A Mandate Is NOT a Law

Distinguishing between mandates and laws can often feel like untangling a web of legalese, especially when these terms are used interchangeably in everyday discourse. The nuances between them hold significant implications for individuals who find themselves navigating workplace policies, public health directives, or governmental orders. This chapter invites readers to delve into the intricate differences and helps clarify what each term entails in practical terms. By shedding light on how mandates and laws operate separately yet sometimes overlap in their effects, we aim to illuminate the path for those affected by such distinctions.

In this chapter, we will explore how mandates and laws differ not only in their formation but also in the weight they carry within legal systems. You'll read about the processes that give laws their binding power compared to the more flexible, often temporary nature of mandates. Moreover, we'll dissect real-world scenarios where these differences matter, providing insights into misinterpretations that have led to unwarranted legal and societal consequences. Through examples and case studies, the chapter illustrates why understanding the distinction is crucial for anyone dealing with employment disputes, healthcare regulations, or civil rights arguments. This exploration will be particularly relevant for employees, healthcare workers, and even families impacted by policy decisions, offering them clarity and guidance on navigating this complex landscape.

Understanding Mandates vs. Laws

Understanding the fundamental differences between mandates and laws is crucial in navigating today's complex social and political landscape. Broadly speaking, a mandate is an official order or commission to perform a specific task. Unlike laws, which are enduring and mandatory, mandates are often temporary and may originate from various levels of government or organizations. They typically aim to address immediate needs with the expectation that they can be adjusted as circumstances evolve. However, their status as non-binding differentiates them markedly from laws.

Laws are constructed through rigorous legislative processes involving debate, discourse, and approval by elected representatives. This process ensures that every law reflects a consensus, securing legal force once it passes through the required channels, ultimately receiving executive sign-off. Compliance with law comes with enforced penalties for violations, reaffirming society's commitment to abiding by shared principles and norms. Laws, thus, stand as pillars of governance, ensuring consistency, accountability, and fairness across the spectrum of societal interactions. In contrast, mandates are not inherently backed by legal enforcement mechanisms, making their authority more situational and context-dependent.

To grasp the significance of mandates, it's essential to recognize how they can function within organizational or governmental contexts. Mandates typically offer guidelines or directives without the weight of law. For example, a government might issue a health mandate requiring citizens to wear masks during a pandemic. While the mandate suggests compliance, breaking it may not carry the same legal repercussions as violating a legislated public health law. The agility of mandates allows them to adapt to changing conditions, serving as flexible tools for authorities. However, this adaptability can lead to confusion if individuals mistakenly equate mandates with laws.

The misunderstanding surrounding mandates stems partly from their presentation. When mandates are communicated, especially by authoritative bodies, they might seem as binding as laws due to tone and language. This perception is compounded when mandates involve conditions that affect everyday life, such as workplace policies or public behavior guidelines. The line blurs further when mandates come with potential consequences tied to federal funding or participation in programs, creating an impression of compulsory adherence similar to that of laws.

Public confusion over mandates versus laws highlights the need for clearer communication and education. Misinterpretation can lead to unnecessary legal disputes or civil disobedience born from resistance to what is perceived as unwarranted intrusion. Misunderstandings might arise in environments where mandates influence critical decisions, like employment conditions or access to services. For instance, employers may enforce company-wide mandates impacting employee rights, assuming mandates have the same legal standing as laws. This misapplication can result in workplace grievances, amplifying tension and mistrust among employees who feel their rights are being overshadowed by policies lacking legislative backing.

Education and transparent communication can mitigate these issues. By clearly defining mandates and distinguishing them from laws, organizations and governments can foster better understanding and cooperation. Comprehensive education campaigns could elucidate when and why mandates are necessary, highlighting their intended scope and limitations. Such efforts would demystify perceptions and ensure adherence aligns with informed consent rather than misplaced obligation.

Furthermore, mandates' susceptibility to change should be acknowledged. As non-permanent measures responsive to evolving contexts, mandates offer a unique advantage, allowing swift adaptations as situations progress. This flexibility makes them practical tools for addressing unforeseen challenges while retaining the capability for adjustment. Yet, this very flexibility necessitates regular review and communication to assure those affected understand any changes to mandates' status or applicability.

The Supreme Court's Intervention

The Supreme Court's decision to review and ultimately strike down OSHA's vaccine mandate marked a significant moment in balancing federal agency authority and individual liberties. Understanding this case illuminates how the Supreme Court functions as a guardian of checks and balances within the U.S. governmental system. It reinforced the notion that while federal agencies like

OSHA have substantial power to regulate workplace safety, there are limits imposed by legal frameworks to check potential overreach.

OSHA, or the Occupational Safety and Health Administration, is tasked with ensuring safe and healthy working conditions by setting and enforcing standards. Historically, it has played a critical role in regulating various workplace hazards, from toxic chemicals to machinery safety. However, the COVID-19 pandemic presented new challenges, prompting OSHA to issue an emergency temporary standard (ETS) requiring large employers to ensure their workers were vaccinated against COVID-19 or tested regularly. This mandate aimed to curb the spread of the virus, which posed a significant threat to public health and workplace safety.

However, the scope and authority of OSHA to enforce such a mandate were called into question. The Supreme Court reviewed whether the agency exceeded its statutory powers under the Occupational Safety and Health Act of 1970. Critics argued that the Act's original intent was to address hazards strictly within the workplace, not those that also exist outside, like a widespread infectious disease. The Court, siding with this interpretation, deemed that OSHA's authority did not extend to implementing broad health mandates without explicit congressional approval. This decision highlighted the importance of delineating where agency powers begin and end, particularly concerning regulations impacting public health at large.

In its ruling, the Supreme Court emphasized the need for clear legislative backing when federal agencies embark on initiatives with sweeping implications. Such measures should ideally be rooted in law passed by Congress, ensuring democratic accountability. This principle guards against unelected officials making consequential decisions that affect millions without direct oversight from elected representatives. The Court's majority opinion reflected concern over allowing agencies to expand their influence unchecked, stressing that only Congress could grant such authority through unambiguous statutes.

This decision underscored the limitations faced by federal agencies like OSHA in their regulatory roles, particularly regarding emerging health threats. By striking down the mandate, the Supreme Court signaled that any expansive regulatory efforts, especially those affecting fundamental rights or imposing significant burdens, require direct congressional authorization. This sentiment resonates with the broader major questions doctrine, which holds that courts should not defer to agency interpretations of law when issues of vast economic and political significance are involved.

The implications of this ruling extend beyond the immediate context of the COVID-19 vaccine mandate. It sets a precedent likely to influence future attempts by federal agencies to impose comprehensive mandates without legislative endorsement. Agencies will need to navigate these judicially imposed boundaries carefully, ensuring their regulations align squarely with statutory provisions. This ruling not only affects OSHA but potentially other agencies with similar regulatory ambitions, compelling them to seek clearer legislative mandates.

For advocates of individual liberties, the decision represents a victory. It reaffirms the principle that significant policy decisions, especially those infringing upon personal freedoms or bodily autonomy, must be deliberated within the legislative branch rather than being enacted through administrative channels. Conversely, some worry about the broader implications for public health management, questioning how effectively agencies can respond to crises if constrained by such legal precedents.

Future agency-driven mandates will likely face heightened scrutiny, and agencies may require more robust legal strategies to justify their actions. This dynamic creates an environment where collaboration between lawmakers and regulators becomes crucial, emphasizing the need for agile yet constitutionally sound responses to evolving challenges.

Misinterpretation by Institutions

In recent times, mandates have been treated by various institutions as laws, creating a landscape fraught with misunderstandings and compliance challenges. Companies, universities, and hospitals, in particular, have frequently enforced these directives with a rigor typically reserved for legally binding legislations. This approach not only muddled the lines between what is mandatory and what is suggested but also led to unforeseen consequences on institutional trust and operational integrity.

Many companies resorted to interpreting mandates as laws due to a mix of caution and misunderstanding. Often, businesses sought to safeguard themselves from potential future liabilities or regulatory backlash by strictly adhering to what they perceived as enforceable rules. However, this could lead to a misdirection where mandates, which are essentially temporary orders or guidelines lacking legal teeth, were upheld with undue stringency. This misstep resulted in confusion among employees, who struggled to understand the boundaries of their obligations, leading to compliance challenges that companies had to navigate without clear legal guidance.

Universities and colleges, striving to protect public health and their campus communities during crises such as the COVID-19 pandemic, adopted mandates affecting both students and staff. These educational institutions imposed strict measures, including mask-wearing, vaccination requirements, and social distancing protocols. While these mandates aimed to maintain a safe learning environment, they often encroached on personal freedoms and blurred the distinction between administrative policies and legal obligations. Students and faculty members frequently faced uncertainties about potential disciplinary actions if they failed to comply, causing friction and debate over the legal basis for such enforcement.

Hospitals and healthcare organizations found themselves at the forefront of mandate interpretations, particularly given their critical role in maintaining public health standards. During health emergencies, many hospitals implemented stringent mandates affecting employment conditions, such as compulsory vaccinations for healthcare workers. While intended to protect patients and ensure uninterrupted care delivery, these mandates raised ethical concerns. The core issue revolved around balancing patient care excellence with respecting personal choice—a dilemma intensified by mandates treated as immutable law. Ethical debates emerged, questioning whether healthcare institutions had the right to impose such mandates without legislative backing, thereby testing the trust between healthcare providers and their employees.

Examining the repercussions of treating mandates as laws reveals significant impacts on institutional trust and operational integrity. Trust within organizations eroded when employees perceived mandates as arbitrary impositions rather than well-justified necessities. This erosion of trust manifested in high rates of employee dissatisfaction, increased turnover, and even legal challenges from those opposing mandated compliance. Institutions struggled to maintain morale and productivity while navigating these complexities.

Furthermore, operational integrity suffered as organizations continuously adapted to evolving mandates. The need to revise plans, procedures, and communication strategies strained resources and diverted attention from core missions. This dynamic environment created uncertainty and inefficiency, hindering long-term planning and execution. Institutions faced the challenge of aligning their strategic goals with mandates, often leading to reactive decision-making instead of proactive leadership.

Institutional trust also extended beyond internal dynamics, impacting external perceptions and relationships. Organizations that appeared to act unilaterally faced reputational damage and skepticism from the public and stakeholders. In some cases, the disconnect between the perception of mandates and their actual legal standing fueled public outcry and backlash, complicating efforts to maintain a harmonious balance between organizational objectives and public accountability.

Addressing these challenges necessitates a careful approach to mandate interpretation and implementation. Institutions must prioritize clear communication, transparency, and stakeholder engagement to build trust and ensure compliance aligns with broader legal frameworks. It requires acknowledging the temporary nature of mandates and avoiding overreach that may infringe upon individual rights and freedoms. By fostering open dialogue, organizations can bridge the gap between mandates and laws, ensuring stakeholders understand the rationale behind measures while preserving operational efficiency and trust.

Employer Overreach and Legal Limits

In today's workplace, the landscape of employment rights is complex and often fraught with tension between company policies and employee protections. Employers frequently establish internal mandates as part of their operational guidelines, aiming to align with organizational goals and ensure streamlined operations. However, such mandates are not absolute and must be carefully balanced against employees' legal rights.

Employers possess the right to set company policies, which might include mandates like dress codes or health-related measures. Nonetheless, they need to tread carefully to avoid infringing on rights that are safeguarded under labor laws and anti-discrimination statutes. These laws form the backbone of employee rights in the workplace, ensuring protection against unfair treatment based on race, gender, disability, age, or other protected characteristics (EEOC, 2024).

To understand the delicate balance employers must navigate, consider the legal challenges associated with terminating employees due to non-compliance with company mandates. For example, if an employee is terminated for refusing a policy-mandated vaccine, the legality hinges on whether such a policy is in direct conflict with established labor laws. Anti-discrimination laws and workplace safety regulations might offer grounds for legal disputes if employees believe their termination was unjust or discriminatory (Best Practices of Private Sector Employers | U.S. Equal Employment Opportunity Commission, n.d.).

Analyzing case studies sheds light on these conflicts. In some cases, courts have intervened where company policies clashed with legal protections. For instance, there have been instances where employees challenged their terminations based on company vaccine mandates, arguing their rights under the Americans with Disabilities Act (ADA) or religious freedom were violated. Courts often weigh the company's rationale for such mandates against employees' legal rights, highlighting the importance of aligning internal policies with external legal frameworks.

Moreover, employers must consider the broader implications of their policies. The effectiveness of a mandate does not just rest on its implementation but also on its alignment with both legal requirements and ethical standards. This dual consideration can help avoid costly legal battles and maintain employee trust and morale.

Best practices for employers involve crafting policies that respect the intricate web of legal obligations while supporting the company's core objectives. A successful approach incorporates clear communication, transparency, and flexibility. Policies should be developed with input from legal experts to ensure compliance with current regulations. Additionally, involving employees in discussions about policy changes can foster a sense of inclusion and commitment, reducing resistance and misunderstandings.

One effective strategy is adopting a collaborative approach similar to the SPLENDID framework proposed by the EEOC, which encourages companies to Study, Plan, Lead, Encourage, Notice, Discuss, Include, and Dedicate efforts towards equal employment opportunities (EEOC, 2024). Such practices not only address legal obligations but also promote a positive workplace culture that values diversity and inclusivity.

Guidelines serve as essential tools for ensuring that employer overreach is curbed and that employee rights are not compromised. It's crucial for employers to understand that while they can implement mandates, they cannot do so at the expense of breaching legally protected rights. Legal counsel and proactive engagement with employees can act as preventive measures against potential violations.

The discussion surrounding employer's rights and limitations is particularly pertinent in today's climate, where issues like vaccine mandates or remote work policies have become focal points. Understanding the legal parameters within which companies can operate is vital for both employers seeking to enforce policies and employees wishing to protect their rights.

Final Insights

In this chapter, we explored the nuanced distinctions between mandates and laws, underscoring their different roles in society. Mandates serve as temporary directives that address immediate needs without the same legal weight as laws, which are formed through comprehensive legislative processes. This discrepancy often leads to misinterpretation when mandates are treated like laws, causing confusion and compliance issues. Misunderstandings are particularly common within institutions like businesses, universities, and healthcare organizations, where mandates are sometimes enforced with a rigor similar to legal statutes. This has resulted in challenges regarding institutional trust and operational effectiveness, as well as broader impacts on public perception.

Clear communication and education are crucial in mitigating these misunderstandings. By defining mandates and distinguishing them from laws, organizations can foster better understanding and cooperation, reducing unnecessary legal conflicts and enhancing adherence out of informed consent rather than mistaken obligation. The adaptability of mandates provides an advantage by allowing swift responses to changing situations. However, recognizing that this flexibility necessitates regular review and transparent communication is vital. This approach ensures those affected understand any changes and helps maintain trust and clarity within both public and institutional contexts.

Reference List

Amanti, L., Snow, K., & Sulaiman, A. (2024, January 1). AHLA - Top Ten Issues in Health Law 2024. Www.americanhealthlaw.org. https://www.americanhealthlaw.org/content-library/connections-magazine/article/d91b2697-e96b-49e4-84c1-1b8399406f5e/Top-Ten-Issues-in-Health-Law

Best Practices of Private Sector Employers | U.S. Equal Employment Opportunity Commission. (n.d.). Www.eeoc.gov. https://www.eeoc.gov/best-practices-private-sector-employers

EEOC. (2024, April 29). Enforcement Guidance on Harassment in the Workplace. US EEOC. https://www.eeoc.gov/laws/guidance/enforcement-guidance-harassment-workplace

FOX43, C. K. (2020, July 7). Political expert explains the difference between a law, order and mandate and if a mask mandate can be enforced. Fox43.com; WPMT. https://www.fox43.com/article/news/local/difference-between-a-law-order-and-mandate-and-can-mandates-orders-be-enforced/521-8a4442ce-5ba5-426e-854c-b7c38ffa0d63

Hughes, A. (2023, July 5). Mandate or Law: The American Founders on Warning Against Arbitrary, Tyrannical Dictates Diluting Rule of Law - Constituting America. Constituting America -. https://constitutingamerica.org/90day-fp-mandate-or-law-the-american-founders-on-warning-against-arbitrary-tyrannical-dictates-diluting-rule-of-law-andrew-langer/

May 17, 2023, & Am, 8:49. (n.d.). The Danger of Applying the Major Questions Doctrine to Major Risks. Vanderbilt University. https://law.vanderbilt.edu/the-danger-of-applying-the-major-questions-doctrine-to-major-risks/

School, S. L. (2022, January 20). A Look at the Supreme Court Ruling on Vaccination Mandates. Stanford Law School. https://law.stanford.edu/2022/01/20/a-look-at-the-supreme-court-ruling-on-vaccination-mandates/

Wolf, D. (2024, September 10). 5 Laws Impacting Healthcare Compliance You Should Know. School of Professional Studies at Wake Forest University. https://sps.wfu.edu/articles/laws-impacting-healthcare-compliance/

Chapter 12 Using New Vaccine Evidence in Your Lawsuit

Leveraging emerging vaccine evidence in legal cases requires a strategic approach. As new findings and testimonies come to light, they can significantly enhance the strength and credibility of legal arguments, particularly for those challenging vaccine mandates. This process involves gathering robust data from various sources—adverse effect reports, expert insights, and statistical analyses—transforming them into compelling pieces of evidence. By focusing on credible information and meticulous documentation, individuals can build a case that stands up to scrutiny in court. It's about using facts and reliable testimonials to support claims and highlight possible injustices related to enforced vaccination policies.

In this chapter, we'll explore how adverse effect reports and notable figures like Robert F. Kennedy Jr. contribute to strengthening legal strategies in vaccine-related lawsuits. We'll delve into the details of leveraging these reports to uncover trends and patterns of side effects and discuss how they can serve as foundational evidence in portraying the potential risks associated with vaccines. Furthermore, the chapter will investigate RFK Jr.'s role in drawing attention to vaccine safety concerns and how his assertions can be integrated into a persuasive legal narrative. We'll also touch upon the importance of statistical correlations in bolstering credibility and how public advocacy efforts can sway jury perceptions. By dissecting these elements, the chapter aims to provide actionable insights for effectively utilizing new vaccine evidence in legal battles against mandates, whether by highlighting recurring issues or illustrating broader implications of policy reversals.

Leveraging Adverse Effect Reports and RFK Jr.'s Insights

In the realm of legal battles surrounding vaccine mandates, grounding your case in substantiated evidence has never been more crucial. A formidable strategy involves leveraging adverse effect reports and insights from figures like Robert F. Kennedy Jr., who has played a pivotal role in drawing attention to potential vaccine-related injuries. This approach not only strengthens your argument but also broadens public awareness about vaccine issues through well-documented evidence and credible testimony.

Begin by delving into adverse effect reports, as these documents are rich with data that highlight trends and patterns of side effects related to vaccines. Such analysis is critical in underscoring the frequency and recurrence of issues faced by individuals who have experienced negative reactions post-vaccination. For instance, these reports may reveal common symptoms such as allergic reactions or neurological impacts following specific vaccinations. By systematically analyzing and presenting these findings, you can build a compelling argument that points to recurring problems within certain vaccines. In this way, these reports become a foundational piece of evidence that underscores the legitimacy of claims regarding vaccine safety concerns.

Moreover, tapping into the research and assertions made by RFK Jr. could bolster your case significantly. His work, albeit controversial to some, provides an avenue for highlighting specific vaccine-related injuries and incidents. RFK Jr.'s advocacy against perceived injustices in vaccine distribution and efficacy offers a narrative that aligns with the experience of those who feel wronged by enforced vaccination policies. Despite debates surrounding his viewpoints, his insights, when corroborated by factual data from adverse effect reports, can serve as a powerful testimonial in court.

Statistical correlations between reported adverse effects and specific vaccines are a vital aspect of establishing credibility in any lawsuit revolving around vaccine mandates. Gathering statistics that demonstrate a direct link between certain vaccines and adverse outcomes strengthens the backbone of your legal arguments. Statistical data acts as an objective measure that courts often rely on to ascertain the validity of a claim. By presenting robust data that correlates specific vaccines with particular health issues, you provide the court with tangible evidence to consider, thereby enhancing the persuasiveness of your case.

It is also important to consider how RFK Jr.'s longstanding advocacy efforts contribute to raising awareness about vaccine-related issues. Over the years, he has tirelessly campaigned to inform the public of potential risks associated with vaccines, thus influencing public opinion and potentially swaying jury perspectives. His ability to garner media attention and provoke public discourse around vaccine safety can add weight to your case by demonstrating a precedent of widespread concern and scrutiny over the matter at hand. In doing so, his advocacy becomes more than just supportive material; it acts as a catalyst for broader discussions about medical freedom and bodily autonomy.

While organizing your legal argument, it's imperative to base claims on verifiable information. This is where the meticulous citation of sources like adverse effect reports and RFK Jr.'s documented statements comes into play. Ensure that every point made is backed by reliable data. For example, in citing adverse effect reports, reference specific studies or databases that validate your claims. When quoting RFK Jr., refer precisely to documented interviews, publications, or speeches where his insights were provided. Such diligent documentation not only prevents challenges from opposing parties but also reinforces the authenticity of your argument.

Additionally, considering the sensitivity of ongoing debates around vaccines, maintaining a balanced tone in court is essential. While it is crucial to assertively present findings from adverse effect reports and RFK Jr.'s advocacy, it is equally important to acknowledge counterarguments respectfully. Doing so demonstrates your preparedness to engage with differing opinions and highlights the thoroughness of your case preparation. By acknowledging various perspectives upfront, you mitigate potential objections and reinforce the overall strength of your position.

Integrating Whistleblower Testimonies into Legal Strategies

Incorporating whistleblower testimonies can significantly strengthen legal claims related to vaccine injuries. Often, whistleblowers provide first-hand accounts and insights that reveal underreported side effects of vaccines, serving as a powerful tool in evidencing claims in court.

The initial step involves collecting testimonies from credible whistleblowers who have firsthand knowledge or evidence about vaccine side effects. These individuals might include healthcare workers, scientists, or former employees with insight into pharmaceutical operations. Their revelations can bring to light side effects that might not have been reported or acknowledged officially.

Once these testimonies are gathered, it is crucial to validate their credibility and authenticity. This process ensures that the testimonies hold up in legal scenarios, making them admissible in court. It requires demonstrating that the whistleblowers have relevant expertise or experience and verifying their accounts with supporting documentation or corroborative testimonies.

Whistleblower narratives often expose inconsistencies or omissions in official reports. For instance, if a pharmaceutical company claims comprehensive reporting on vaccine side effects, but a whistleblower discloses otherwise, this disparity can be pivotal. Such revelations can undermine official statements, raising questions about transparency and integrity in vaccine reporting.

Moreover, the impact of whistleblower testimonies extends beyond the courtroom. Public perception is often influenced by these firsthand accounts, as they provide relatable, humanized experiences that statistics alone cannot convey. Jury members, being part of the general populace, may respond sympathetically to these personal stories. Whistleblower testimonies can evoke emotional responses that statistical data might not, potentially swaying jury views towards favoring plaintiffs' arguments about vaccine injuries.

It's important to note that public reaction to whistleblower accounts can vary based on social media amplification and individual biases. As outlined by Fritz & Smith (2025), personal testimonies can elicit stronger reactions than other types of evidence because they tap into emotional and empathetic facets of human nature. The emotional weight carried by whistleblower stories can amplify their effect in legal contexts, especially when the public has preconceived notions about vaccine safety or skepticism of authority figures.

To strategically use whistleblower testimonies in legal proceedings, it's essential to present them within a broader framework of evidence. They should complement adverse effect reports, scientific studies, and expert opinions to create a cohesive argument. This synthesis not only strengthens legal cases but also anticipates potential counterarguments by building an evidence base that is difficult to dismiss outright.

Guidelines for utilizing whistleblower testimonies effectively involve thorough preparation and strategic presentation. Attorneys should ensure that testimonies are clear, concise, and directly relevant to the case at hand. Furthermore, preparing the whistleblower for cross-examinations is vital, as opposing counsel will likely attempt to challenge their credibility or motives.

Drawing from the experiences of whistleblowers can also highlight the broader implications of vaccine side effects. For example, if a whistleblower reveals a pattern of side effects previously undocumented, it could indicate systemic issues within vaccine reporting mechanisms. This revelation could prompt further inquiries or regulatory changes, illustrating the significant ripple effects that single testimonies can initiate.

Additionally, understanding the influence of social media on public sentiment and legal outcomes is crucial. According to Cascini et al. (2022), social media's role as an intervention platform means that whistleblower testimonies shared online could reach a vast audience quickly. These platforms can both bolster and challenge narratives, influencing potential jurors who form part of the engaged public.

Proving Unjust Mandates with Military Reinstatement Orders

In recent years, the military's handling of COVID-19 vaccine mandates has become a compelling narrative in legal discussions surrounding vaccination policies. The decision to reinstate service members who were discharged for refusing the COVID-19 vaccine provides a poignant look into how initial mandates are being reconsidered, presenting an avenue to argue against similar civil vaccine mandates.

The reinstatement orders represent a significant shift in the stance of military authorities, marking a reassessment of initial decisions regarding vaccine requirements. This change can be seen as an implicit acknowledgment that previous mandates may have been overly stringent or not entirely justified. These actions could serve as potent evidence in lawsuits challenging the fairness and legality of civil vaccine mandates. In fact, such military precedents can be powerful tools when arguing against civilian mandates, as they highlight the flexibility and willingness of a structured organization like the military to adapt its policies in light of new evidence or perspectives.

Examining these orders closely reveals a deeper understanding of the implications of policy reversals. Military decisions often set benchmarks for broader societal norms; thus, when the military decides to reverse a mandate, it sends ripples across various sectors. This development implies that broader societal mandates could also be subject to reevaluation and ultimately reversal. Legal arguments can leverage this to encourage a reconsideration of civil vaccination mandates, underscoring that if the military finds room for reversal, so too should other institutions.

Highlighting discrepancies between civilian and military vaccination policies further strengthens legal arguments against mandates. While civilians faced job loss due to non-compliance, military personnel are being reinstated with full back pay, benefits, and compensation. This inconsistency highlights a double standard that civilian employees might argue against in court. If the military, known for its rigorous requirements, is revisiting its approach, it challenges the notion that civilian mandates should remain unchanged. The contrasting policies can be pivotal in shaping legal narratives emphasizing unfair treatment between sectors.

Moreover, the military's actions underscore the broader, long-term implications for mandate compliance at large. Those seeking redress for wrongful terminations or facing undue pressure to comply with mandates under duress can point to these developments. They provide a basis for arguing that civil mandates lack permanence and are susceptible to change, much like their military counterparts. Such shifts invite scrutiny into whether mandates truly align with current health priorities or simply reflect outdated policies.

For plaintiffs, it's crucial to use clear examples from these military precedents to craft robust legal arguments. By thoroughly examining the rationale behind the reinstatements, one can draw parallels to civil contexts, illustrating how mandates may conflict with evolving public health strategies. This alignment can showcase that while the intent behind mandates might be protective, their enforcement must consider fairness and adaptability.

In discussing legal strategies, these points open doors to question the rigid interpretation of mandates in civilian employment. Attorneys can capitalize on these military insights by highlighting the potential for alternative approaches to achieving public health goals without resorting to punitive measures. It encourages a dialogue about proportional responses to public health crises, especially considering personal autonomy and informed choice.

Service members' reinstatement serves as a testament to the changing landscape of mandate policies, providing essential case studies for legal professionals advocating for wrongfully terminated individuals. These cases reflect on the appropriateness of mandates and encourage a thoughtful reconsideration that goes beyond simple compliance to respect individual rights and freedoms within societal structures.

Synthesizing Evidence for a Cohesive Legal Argument

In the shifting landscape of legal battles over vaccine mandates, crafting a potent argument hinges on effectively synthesizing diverse sources of evidence. This begins with weaving together adverse effect reports, whistleblower testimonies, and military reinstatement orders to form a coherent narrative that highlights the multifaceted impacts of these mandates.

Adverse effect reports can serve as a foundation for establishing a pattern or trend related to vaccine complications. These reports, which detail instances of side effects following vaccination, are vital for illustrating potential risks and reinforcing claims of harm. By analyzing these reports comprehensively, one can pinpoint recurring issues and showcase a broader spectrum of vaccine-related challenges. For instance, identifying clusters of similar adverse reactions across different demographics could underline the consistency and severity of observed problems.

Whistleblower testimonies can add another layer of credibility and insight into the conversation. These individuals often expose underreporting of side effects or internal discord within organizations, providing an insider perspective that is both compelling and persuasive. Ensuring the authenticity and reliability of these testimonials is crucial, as they not only bolster the adverse effect data but also provide firsthand accounts that humanize the legal arguments. In these cases, cross-referencing whistleblower accounts with documented incidents can amplify their impact.

Military reinstatement orders offer additional evidence of the reconsideration of vaccine policies, suggesting a recognition of potential pitfalls in initial decisions. These orders demonstrate tangible government responses to previous mandates, which can be pivotal when arguing against the fairness and legality of civilian vaccine requirements. By examining such precedents, one can argue that if a branch as structured as the military can reassess its stance, there might be merit in reevaluating mandates applied to the general populace.

Synthesizing these elements demands a strategic approach to presentation in court. An effective strategy involves preemptively addressing potential counterarguments, thereby strengthening the case's foundation. By anticipating weaknesses, such as questioning the validity of adverse effect data or the motives behind whistleblower narratives, one can fortify arguments with comprehensive analytics and corroborative evidence. Incorporating extensive data analysis, expert testimonies, and robust documentation can help mitigate anticipated critiques, ensuring a resilient defense against opposing viewpoints.

A unified legal strategy should culminate from this synthesis, using all available evidence cohesively. Presenting a well-rounded argument entails integrating each source's strengths, whether it's the statistical backing of adverse reports, the emotional gravity of whistleblower accounts, or the regulatory implications suggested by military orders. This comprehensive approach not only appeals to factual scrutiny but also resonates on an ethical level, highlighting broader implications of mandate repercussions.

While constructing this narrative, it is important to maintain clarity and precision, avoiding unnecessary complexity that might alienate the audience or obscure the case's essence. The goal is to create a relatable and understandable argument that reflects the experiences and concerns of affected employees and advocates for policy change. Using plain language and logical progression, the narrative should guide the audience through the evidence clearly and compellingly.

Summary and Reflections

In this chapter, we've explored how emerging vaccine evidence can be a game-changer in strengthening legal arguments. By examining adverse effect reports and drawing insights from figures like RFK Jr., we see that data and personal narratives can significantly impact court cases. When whistleblower testimonies reveal inconsistencies in official reports, they add a human element that's hard to ignore. Meanwhile, the military's decision to reinstate service members demonstrates how policies can shift in light of new evidence. These elements together provide a powerful framework for those challenging vaccine mandates.

For wrongfully terminated employees and others affected by these mandates, understanding these strategies is key to building a compelling case. The combination of factual data and firsthand accounts forms a robust argument against the perceived injustices of enforced vaccination policies. This chapter encourages you to consider these multidimensional approaches when questioning the legality and fairness of such mandates. As these discussions continue to evolve, staying informed about new findings will empower you to navigate the legal landscape effectively.

Reference List

Berke, R. (2025, January 28). Private emails show RFK Jr. making false claims about Covid-19 shots, linking vaccines to autism. STAT. https://www.statnews.com/2025/01/28/kennedy-confirmation-hearing-niece-releases-emails-vaccine-criticism-conspiracy-theories/

Cascini, F., Pantovic, A., Al-Ajlouni, Y. A., Failla, G., Puleo, V., Melnyk, A., Lontano, A., & Ricciardi, W. (2022, May). Social media and attitudes towards a COVID-19 vaccination: A systematic review of the literature. EClinicalMedicine. https://doi.org/10.1016/j.eclinm.2022.101454

Cole, D. (2021, September 2). ACLU News & Commentary. American Civil Liberties Union. https://www.aclu.org/news/civil-liberties/civil-liberties-and-vaccine-mandates-heres-our-take

Executive Order Tracker. (2025, January 24). Littler Mendelson P.C. https://www.littler.com/publication-press/publication/executive-order-tracker

Fritz, A. M., & Smith, A. M. (2025, January 3). Poison, lies, war: A mixed methods content analysis of posts about COVID-19 vaccination on Gab Social. Human Vaccines & Immunotherapeutics; Taylor & Francis. https://doi.org/10.1080/21645515.2024.2443999

Hostile Work Environment: Guide for Whistleblowers - National Whistleblower Center. (2025, January 10). National Whistleblower Center. https://www.whistleblowers.org/whistleblower-resources/hostile-work-environment-guide-for-whistleblowers/

Yandell, C. J., Kate. (2023, August 11). RFK Jr.'s COVID-19 Deceptions. FactCheck.org. https://www.factcheck.org/2023/08/scicheck-rfk-jr-s-covid-19-deceptions/

admin_pwd. (2024, January 19). Whistleblower Retaliation Claims Guide | PBW Law. Pearlman, Brown & Wax. https://www.pbw-law.com/the-anatomy-of-whistleblower-retaliation-claims-what-employers-need-to-know/

If you were fired under a vaccine mandate, now is the time to take action. **Use the legal system to make them pay.**

Don't miss out!

Visit the website below and you can sign up to receive emails whenever Wayne C. Robinson publishes a new book. There's no charge and no obligation.

https://books2read.com/r/B-A-TOYXD-THJRG

BOOKS 2 READ

Connecting independent readers to independent writers.

Did you love *COVID 19 Lawsuits: How to Sue Your Employer And Win*? Then you should read *The Hulda Clark Story*[1] by Wayne C. Robinson!

[2]

The Hulda Clark Story*The Truth They Didn't Want You To Know*By Wayne C. Robinson

What if the cure for cancer, AIDS, and dozens of chronic illnesses had already been discovered—but was systematically silenced?

This gripping exposé uncovers the untold story of Dr. Hulda Regehr Clark, a brilliant yet controversial scientist, naturopath, and researcher who claimed to have found the root causes of nearly all diseases—and the means to cure them. Her conclusions challenged the foundation of modern medicine, threatening the multi-billion-dollar pharmaceutical and healthcare industries.

Dr. Clark identified parasites, toxins, and pollutants as the true culprits behind most illnesses and designed a series of detox protocols and a revolutionary electronic device called the *Zapper* to eliminate them. With thousands of testimonials from patients around the world, her books—*The*

1. https://books2read.com/u/3GZV08

2. https://books2read.com/u/3GZV08

Cure for All Diseases, The Cure for HIV and AIDS, and others—became global underground bestsellers, offering hope to those failed by conventional treatments.

But that hope came at a cost.

The medical establishment, backed by powerful regulatory agencies and corporate interests, launched an aggressive campaign to discredit and destroy her work. From legal harassment and smear campaigns to the sudden shutdown of her clinics, Dr. Clark's research was buried beneath a mountain of institutional resistance. At one point, she was even arrested in the United States for "practicing medicine without a license"—despite having treated patients successfully across borders.

In *The Hulda Clark Story*, investigative journalist Wayne C. Robinson draws on interviews, official records, insider documents, and Dr. Clark's own writings to reconstruct her extraordinary life and the forces that conspired to silence her. He reveals:

How Dr. Clark discovered a pattern behind all diseases—and how to reverse themThe detailed steps of her groundbreaking protocols, including parasite cleansing, detoxification, and frequency healingThe stories of patients who credit her with saving their lives after being declared incurableWhy the FDA, media, and mainstream medical authorities labeled her a fraud—and the real reason behind their campaignThe ongoing efforts to revive her legacy and share her findings with a new generation of truth-seekers

This book is not just a biography—it's a call to awaken.

In an age where censorship and medical conformity threaten open inquiry, *The Hulda Clark Story* stands as a powerful testament to courage, truth, and the right to choose your path to wellness. Whether you're a skeptic or a believer, this story will make you question everything you think you know about disease, health, and the real powers that shape our world.

If you've ever wondered why natural cures are hidden, discredited, or banned—this book will open your eyes.

Read more at www.enemieswithinus.com.

Also by Wayne C. Robinson

Enemies Within Us
The Hulda Clark Story
The USAID Scandal: How Billions Disappeared
Why Black Americans No Longer Need DEI
USAID And Child Trafficking
COVID 19 Lawsuits: How to Sue Your Employer And Win
America is $37 Trillion in Debt
Unfit to lead– The End of The Democratic Party
Black Fatigue
The Red Shift: Communism in The U.S.
The 2025 Real State of Black America
Die Hulda Clark Story
The Job Hunt is a Scam: Here's How to Beat It
The Sanctuary City Scam And Black Americans
The Global Black MLM Trap
2026 The Year the Democratic Party Collapses
The Global Black MLM/Network Marketing Trap
Faith, Migration & Power
Lifestyle Red Alert

Everything About Timeshares
Cancel Your Timeshare Today
Everything About Timeshares (2025 Edition)

The Tandem Methods™
She is Africa

Watch for more at www.enemieswithinus.com.

www.ingramcontent.com/pod-product-compliance
Lightning Source LLC
LaVergne TN
LVHW050819061126
851857LV00012B/883
* 9 7 9 8 2 3 1 4 5 5 4 2 3 *